FABIAN
SOCIETY

The Fabian Society is Britain's oldest political think tank. Since 1884 the society has played a central role in developing political ideas and public policy on the left.

Through a wide range of publications and events the society influences political and public thinking, but also provides a space for broad and open-minded debate, drawing on an unrivalled external network and its own expert research and analysis.

The society is alone among think tanks in being a democratically-constituted membership organisation, with over 7,000 members. During its history the membership has included many of the key thinkers on the British left and every Labour prime minister. Today it counts over 200 parliamentarians in its number. Member-led activity includes 70 local Fabian societies, the Scottish and Welsh Fabians, the Fabian Women's Network and the Young Fabians, which is itself the leading organisation on the left for young people to debate and influence political ideas.

The society was one of the original founders of the Labour party and is constitutionally affiliated to the party. It is however editorially, organisationally and financially independent and works with a wide range of partners of all political persuasions and none.

Fabian Society
61 Petty France
London SW1H 9EU
www.fabians.org.uk

Fabian Ideas 643

First published 2017
ISBN 978-0-7163-0643-6

Head of editorial: Kate Murray

British Library Cataloguing in Publication data. A catalogue
record for this book is available from the British Library.

Printed and bound by DG3, London, UK

To find out more about the Fabian Society, the Young
Fabians, the Fabian Women's Network and our local
societies, please visit our website at www.fabians.org.uk

This Woman Can

1997, women and Labour

Edited by Sally Keeble

Acknowledgements

This publication would not have been possible without generous donations from:

Heidi Alexander, Charlotte Atkins, Luciana Berger, Liz Blackman, Tessa Blackstone, Hazel Blears, Anne Campbell, Mary Creagh, Ann Cryer, Claire Curtis-Thomas, Janet Dean, Caroline Flint, Linda Gilroy, Eileen Gordon, Joyce Gould, Nia Griffith, Sylvia Heal, Bev Hughes, Helen Jackson, Melanie Johnson, Tessa Jowell, Sally Keeble, Ann Keen, Ruth Kelly, Jane Kennedy, Helen Liddell, Fiona Mactaggart, Judy Mallaber, Siobhain McDonagh, Rosemary McKenna, Gillian Merron, Laura Moffatt, Julie Morgan, Estelle Morris, Meg Munn, Linda Perham, Bridget Prentice, Margaret Prosser, Joyce Quin, Jan Royall, Joan Ryan, Angela Smith, Phyllis Starkey, Gisela Stuart, Claire Ward, Lynda Waltho.

This publication was also supported by Community.

community
For a better working world

We also acknowledge the kind support of Labour Women's Network

Labour Women's Network exists to secure the election of more Labour women to public office at every level and to support Labour women to play a full part in the party.

LWN was founded in 1988 by four Labour women: Barbara Follett, Barbara Roche, Hilary De Lyon and Jean Black. They wanted to change the Labour party and get more women into parliament as Labour MPs. LWN played a key role in the campaign for positive action to get more women selected as Labour candidates in winnable seats.

LWN continues to campaign for women's power and agency in the party. While women make up more than half of Labour's membership, we are absent from leadership positions across our party, abuse and intimidation is commonplace, and BAME, disabled, working class and LGBT women are underrepresented in our ranks.

We are campaigning to deliver the rule change and culture change we need to ensure all Labour women can lead. Our Time to Lead campaign is:

- Calling for our party leadership to keep its promise for 50:50 representation at every level of the party
- Asking for all party members to take our #powerpledge to share their power
- Training the next generation of women change makers

Want to help? Visit www.lwn.org.uk/timetolead and play your part.

About the authors

Dame Vera Baird QC was a barrister before being elected as MP for Redcar in 2001. She served as a justice minister and solicitor general. She is now Police and Crime Commissioner for Northumbria.

Dame Margaret Beckett MP was first elected as MP for Lincoln in October 1974, and for Derby South in 1983. She was elected the party's first woman deputy leader in 1992 and served as leader following the death of John Smith. She was the first, and only, woman foreign secretary.

Dame Anne Begg served as MP for Aberdeen South between 1997 and 2015. She chaired the work and pensions select committee and was vice chair of the speaker's conference to look at the lack of diversity in the House of Commons.

Yvette Cooper MP was elected to represent Pontefract and Castleford in 1997. She has held a wide variety of government posts, and served in the Cabinet between 2008 and 2010. She presently chairs the home affairs select committee.

Angela Eagle MP was elected to represent Wallasey in 1992. She has served in Labour governments between 1997 and 2002, and then returned to the front bench in 2007. After 2010 she served in the shadow cabinet.

Caroline Flint MP was elected to represent Don Valley in 1997. Between 2003 and 2009 she held a range of ministerial positions. In opposition she served as shadow communities secretary and shadow energy secretary.

Harriet Harman MP QC was elected to represent Peckham in 1992 and was appointed to the frontbench 10 years later. She has served in a number of roles both in government and in opposition. She was elected deputy leader of the Labour party in 2008, and served twice as interim leader.

Dame Margaret Hodge MP has represented Barking since 1994. She started her political career as a member, and then leader of Islington council. She served in a number of ministerial roles while Labour was in government, including as the first ever minister for children.

Sharon Hodgson MP represents Washington and Sunderland West. First elected in 2005, she was appointed as government whip in 2009. In opposition she has served as shadow children's minister and shadow public health minister.

Sally Keeble served as an MP for Northampton North from 1997 to 2010. She served as minister for transport, local government and the regions, and then the department for international development.

Liz Kendall MP has been MP for Leicester West since 2010 after being special advisor to the health secretary Patricia Hewitt. She was appointed to the front bench by Ed Miliband as shadow minister for care and older people.

Shabana Mahmood MP a former barrister, was elected as MP for Birmingham Ladywood in 2010. She served as shadow minister in the Home Office, business and Treasury teams and is now on the international trade committee.

Fiona Mactaggart MP was elected to represent Slough in 1997. She served as a minister in the Home Office and was a long-standing chair of the parliamentary Labour party's women's committee.

Siobhain McDonagh MP was first elected to represent her home constituency of Mitcham and Morden in 1997. She served as an assistant whip and on a number of committees, most recently the women's and equalities.

Laura Moffatt was MP for Crawley from 1997 to 2010 and served as a ministerial aide. She worked as a nurse before and after her time in parliament, and began her political career on Crawley council.

Lisa Nandy MP was elected to represent Wigan in 2010. She joined the frontbench in 2012, and was appointed shadow secretary of state for energy and climate change in 2015 and is now on the education select committee.

Frances O'Grady became the first woman general secretary of the Trade Union Congress in January 2013, previously working for the Transport and General Workers Union. She is a commissioner on the government's commission for employment and skills.

Jess Phillips MP was elected to represent Birmingham Yardley in 2015. She has served as an aide to a shadow cabinet member, and is presently the chair of the parliamentary Labour party's women's committee.

Paula Sherriff MP was elected to represent Dewsbury in 2015. As a new MP she led a successful campaign for the abolition of VAT on sanitary products and became to first MP in history to have an amendment made to a Budget resolution.

Tulip Siddiq MP has represented Hampstead and Kilburn since the 2015 general election. She has served on the women and equalities select committee and was shadow minister for early years.

Jacqui Smith was MP for Redditch from 1997 until 2010. She was a schools minister, government chief whip and in 2007 was appointed as the first woman home secretary. She is chair of University Hospitals Birmingham NHS Foundation Trust.

CONTENTS

This pamphlet is about the transformation of politics by Labour women. The 418 Labour MPs elected in 1997 kicked out a Tory government. The 101 of us who were women also transformed our politics. Until that election, parliament had been a largely male preserve and that distorted public policy. We had a welfare state based on male living and working patterns, while many children and pensioners, especially women, were living in poverty. Our economy was hampered by skills shortages, while many women of working age were trapped at home by a lack of affordable childcare or a dysfunctional benefits system. Little was done about a preventable cause of death among women – domestic violence.

So getting more women elected as MPs wasn't just an end in itself, important though it was to have a parliament that looked more like the country it represented. It was also about policy, and some of the benefits are set out in this pamphlet: changes in pensions, healthcare, childcare, equality extended to all, and an economy that worked for the many – women included – and not just the few, with enough to spare to fight the scourge of global poverty.

We women MPs who entered parliament that day stood on the shoulders of giants of the trade union and Labour move-ment: Annie Besant, Mary Macarthur, Margaret Bondfield, Eleanor Marx, Jennie Lee, Barbara Castle and Jo Richardson.

Some of the giants are in parliament still and have contributed to this book: Harriet Harman, Margaret Beckett and Angela Eagle. Diane Abbott was the first, and for many years the only, woman MP from Britain's black communities.

We also paved the way for a new generation of women MPs who are redefining Labour values in changing and contentious times. Some of them – Lisa Nandy, Paula Sherriff and Tulip Siddiq – have also contributed to this pamphlet. The greater diversity of the new intake is important as black and minority ethnic women have carried a double burden of discrimination.

One face in the 2015 intake will be forever missing: Jo Cox who inspired us with her dynamic commitment and was so cruelly murdered.

In looking at the achievements of Labour women in parliament, we must remember that we would never have got there without the support and solidarity from women and men across the Labour movement.

Labour women MPs elected in 1992 had to endure the same hostility that was unleashed with such venom on their successors, and that continues viscerally through social media today. Yet the work that they did through the first women's committee of the parliamentary Labour party, co-chaired by Jean Corston and Helen Jackson, was crucial in achieving change.

Having supported all-women shortlists, the trade unions provided invaluable training, financial and logistical support to prepare Labour women activists for selections, as did Labour Women's Network and Emily's List established by Barbara Follett.

So we are a movement, a historic sweep of humanity, with justice on our side. Since 1997 other parties have wrestled to get more women elected as MPs. In the devolved legislatures, gender equality is expected. Questions are asked if women aren't on the frontbench, in cabinet, or in Number 10. Politics can never go back to how it was. The three of us who were there 20 years ago have worked together on this pamphlet to mark the legacy of that election victory.

But, we're not there yet, as Jess Phillips so effectively argues in her conclusion. There's still a way to go to feminise our public policy and our body politic. We need more Labour women at the grassroots, in local government, parliament and in our party's leadership. And somewhere out there is the woman who will become the first woman Labour prime minister.

Caroline Flint MP
Siobhain McDonagh MP
Sally Keeble

INTRODUCTION

Harriet Harman MP

May 1 this year marks the 20th anniversary of the day when 101 Labour women MPs were elected to parliament and transformed not only the face of parliament but the agenda of politics and the work of government.

That day marked the culmination of over 20 years of work by Labour women to change the Labour party to make it electable, to change parliament to make it properly representative and to change government to make it act in the interests of women as well as men.

Parliament was not representative because it was overwhelmingly male. When I was elected in 1982, only 3 per cent of MPs were women and I was one of only 10 Labour women MPs. Women's voices were not heard in parliament and women in the country could not see their concerns reflected on the political agenda.

And Labour could not get elected because we could not win the votes of women. They saw us as a male-dominated party representing only male manual workers in our traditional industrial heartlands.

Labour women wanted our party to change so that it could reflect our principles of belief in equality for all and our commitment to tackle discrimination. But we also pressed for the advance of women in the Labour party as we knew it was key to helping us get elected. So long as Labour remained male-dominated, women would be reluctant to vote for us and we would continue to languish in opposition, unable to end the suffering which was being caused by Thatcher's government.

We believed that we needed to do three things: transform our policy agenda so that it reflected women's concerns and aspirations, get more women elected as Labour MPs and ensure that Labour's front bench team included women as well as men.

The women's movement which had been growing strongly since the early 1970s had a well-defined policy agenda. We wanted childcare to be recognised as a basic service necessary for the children of working women. Women were going out to work yet a nursery place was only available for children who were at risk. We wanted domestic violence to be recognised for the serious violent crime that it is. This was a time when a woman who was beaten by her husband was deemed to have 'brought it on herself'. We wanted legal rights to enable women to combine their work and their family responsibilities, with protection for part-timers and increased maternity pay and leave. Both their role in the workplace and their role in the family needed to be recognised and supported. We wanted equal pay at work to be a reality not just a theoretical right.

So over the course of the 1980s, we embarked on a process of engaging with women, in women's groups, at work, in community organisations, in local government and in all parts of the country, to listen to them and to discuss how we could take their concerns to the heart of Labour's policy agenda and into government. We were accused of being narrow in our political concerns and of "banging on" about women. But we knew that this was what women wanted and that it was necessary to get us elected.

We knew that however good our policies for women were, women would be less likely to listen to them if they were only talked about by men. We needed women to be at the heart of Labour decision-making and prominent in presenting our policies. The overwhelming majority of Labour MPs were men and there was only one woman in the shadow cabinet. We began by arguing for a woman to be on every shortlist where a Labour MP was retiring. That was controversial and seen as hostile to men. But although the rule change was made, bringing an end to all-male short-lists which had been the norm, it was still the men who got selected to replace male Labour MPs. So we argued for half of those on shortlists to be women. Again that was controversial, and, again, it failed to get women selected. So we argued for half the seats where men were retiring and half the seats we hoped to win to be reserved for women and for men not to be able to apply. This was hugely divisive within the party and criticised as discriminatory and an infringement of the rights of local parties to choose the candidate they wanted. But it went through Labour's conference in 1993 and paved the way for there to be Labour women candidates in every region of England and in Scotland and in Wales who then went on to win in 1997.

It was not, though, enough just to have women as candidates. We needed women to be leading spokespersons for the party and in the shadow cabinet. At that time the parliamentary Labour party voted for the shadow cabinet and only one woman was elected, Jo Richardson, who was our women's spokesperson. We argued for there to be a minimum of four women in the shadow cabinet and in order to minimise the opposition to it within the PLP, extra places were to be added. But despite the fact that there would be no fewer places for men, only extra places for women, the change was bitterly contested, being dubbed "the tarts' charter" by angry Labour male MPs. But at the insistence of our then leader, Neil Kinnock, the move was pushed through the PLP and more women joined the shadow cabinet.

By 1997, women could see that our party had been transformed. We had a fully formed woman-friendly policy agenda, 100 women candidates in seats we were set to win and women in the shadow cabinet ready to take their place in the cabinet. This had taken over 20 years to achieve – but it was a massive change.

The arrival of the women in parliament on May 1 1997 was to be the start of a whole swathe of changes to back women up in their changing lives. Most of the women in the PLP were new, having been elected for the first time in 1997. The senior echelons of the party and the government were still male as were the top civil servants and the political advisors. But over the years that followed the women Labour MPs of 1997 gained experience, became junior ministers and then cabinet members and more women were appointed as special advisors and to the senior ranks of the civil service. And as that happened, our agenda for change for women gathered pace.

By the time we left office, having lost the general election in 2010, government had transformed the support for women in their work and family lives. We had introduced the national childcare strategy, with children's centres in every community. In my own constituency, as all around the country, the number of nursery places more than doubled. We doubled maternity pay and leave and introduced paternity pay and leave for the first time. We brought in a right to request flexible working and strengthened protection for part-time workers. We increased the support for carers of elderly and disabled relatives. We brought in new laws on domestic violence and strengthened the support for victims. We brought in a national minimum wage which was the biggest increase in women's pay since the Equal Pay Act had come into force in 1975. We topped up the income of low-paid women with tax credits and we abolished the poverty of women who didn't have the basic state pension with a minimum income guarantee for pensioners. And we laid the basis for further progress with the 2010 Equality Act.

Now we live, once again, under a Tory government which means that progress for women is stalling and there is a threat that the clock will be turned back. There are protests all around the country as children's centres are cut back, tax credits cut and support for victims of domestic violence reduced. We have a woman prime minister but she does not lead for progress in the lives of women in this country. That role, as ever, falls to the Labour party, to our 100 Labour women MPs, our strong network of women councillors and party members, and we will not shrink from that task.

1: THE ECONOMY:
FROM WALLET TO PURSE

Yvette Cooper MP and Shabana Mahmood MP

Making the economy work for women as well as men was a huge priority for the Labour government in 1997 and beyond. But in the last few years, the economic clock has been turned back. We now need concerted action once more to create an economy that is fair for all.

The challenge

Shifting economic power from wallet to purse was one of the biggest challenges facing the new Labour government in 1997.

As part of Labour's plans for economic growth, investing in public services and tackling poverty, we believed a strong economy involved empowering women, and tackling the historic gender inequality in incomes and opportunities.

Within two years we had already achieved quantifiable results. The Treasury calculated that Labour's first budget had been twice as good for women as for men. Women had benefited on average by £5.30 a week, and men by £2.30.

When we left office the onward progress of economic equality was put into sharp reverse by the Tory-led coalition and then the Conservative government. In 2012, just two years into the coalition government, the House of Commons

Library calculated that its first budgets had directly hit women three times as hard as men.

Stark figures. But they show why women benefited from having a Labour government that included in its ranks so many more women. They also show why it is so important that Labour once again champions women's equality for a new generation.

For Labour, entering government in 1997 was a historic moment after 18 years of Tory rule. For the Labour women MPs elected it was a watershed: doubling the number of women in parliament, cracking the 100 barrier for the first time, and challenging centuries of parliamentary domination of men. Labour women had been battling in parliament for decades to progress women's economic equality: from Margaret Bondfield's efforts to improve women's rights at work, to Barbara Castle's herculean role in ensuring equal pay and much more.

But these had only scratched the surface of long-standing structural economic inequalities. Under Tory governments, Britain's economic and social model had remained frozen in post-war stereotypes of male earners and female care-givers. During the 80s and early 90s, child and pensioner poverty had soared – with lone parents and older pensioners, predominantly women, the hardest hit. Women made up a disproportionate number of the poorest groups in society. Childcare provision was patchy and expensive, parental leave and rights were limited, and little was being done to tackle discrimination or unequal pay.

And the result was an economy failing to make the most of women's skills and talents, an outrageous combination of circumstances. It affected the whole country, which suffered from cycles of high domestic inflation alternating with high unemployment, social exclusion, and child poverty following poor macroeconomic policy, waves of deindustrialisation and low public investment by the Tory governments in the 1980s and 1990s.

That was the background against which more Labour women than ever entered parliament in 1997, part of a new Labour government committed to make the economy work for the many not the few.

Achievements of the Labour government

Alongside macroeconomic changes like Bank of England independence and new fiscal rules to stabilise the economy, Labour boosted investment in infrastructure and skills. We also planned to reform the labour market and tackle poverty – and empowering women formed a big part of that.

For a start, it meant making it possible for women to participate in the economy. Labour argued that work was the best route out of poverty and that the economy should be able to draw on everyone's talents, and that women and men should be better able to balance work and family life. The party's policy-making was underpinned by more modern ideas about gender, recognising that women's role ought to be in employment as much as parenting, and that women needed support to balance their traditional childcare duties with work.

The result was a raft of practical measures: the first ever national childcare strategy with free nursery education, financial support so women could afford childcare, tax relief for employers, and a massive expansion in the number of childcare places. This is set out in more detail in chapter 3 on childcare.

We brought in changes to rights at work – extending paid maternity leave from 18 weeks to 39 weeks by 2010 with up to three months unpaid leave for all parents. We expanded that even further, delivering equal rights for part-time workers to make it easier for parents balancing work and family life.

The new deal for lone parents provided substantial training and childcare support to provide pathways for lone parents to enter the workplace, lifting hundreds of thousands of children out of poverty as a result. Britain's lone parents had languished near the bottom of the European league table for employment, with under a half employed in 1997. By 2010 that figure was nearer two-thirds.

The national minimum wage especially benefited women who predominated then – as now – in the lower paid jobs.

But above all it was tax credits that made work pay for everyone and supported incomes for the lowest paid households, many of which were headed by women.

The story of tax credits shows clearly why it made a real difference having so many women in parliament. Labour women MPs spotted that, under the Treasury's original proposals, tax credits would have been paid to the main earner rather than the main carer. Because men tended to be the main earners in their households the result would have been a direct shift from 'purse to wallet'. It would inadvertently have widened the gap between women and men. Labour women raised the alarm and got the plans changed when the child tax credit was introduced in 2003.

Part of the tax credit regime were childcare tax credits. These were the first time that any government had recognised the true cost of childcare to working women, and provided the flexibility to pay for the kind of childcare needed to for women doing shift work. It enabled women to claim back up to 70 per cent of approved childcare costs, up to £100 for one child or £150 for two or more children when it was introduced in 1997. By 2003, 167,000 families were receiving this support to meet their childcare costs.

Labour response to recession

A decade of unprecedented economic growth for the UK came to an end in 2008 with the financial crash that started in the USA's mortgage market and spread around the world. It was fuelled by an out of control international financial sector, and the failure of financial regulation both here and overseas. The ensuing recession had a profound impact on working people who experienced cuts in working hours or pay rates.

Government action to support the economy stopped the banking system from collapsing, supported key industries, and stopped unemployment reaching the heights of previous recessions. Temporary VAT cuts helped support the economy and keep down prices. Public sector borrowing and debt rose to support households and the economy at a difficult time.

The consequences for men and women were different: the number of women in work grew by more than 250,000 during the recession years, while employment among men fell by 70,000. This was in part a measure of the continuing gender disparity in pay.

People also changed their working hours, family arrangements and lifestyles to pull together and get through. And the tax credits brought in during good times to make work pay and tackle poverty proved a vital cushion in bad times to support family income and the economy as hours and wages were cut. It was the Tory government's attempt to dismantle tax credits in the autumn of 2015 that produced the first serious rebellion among its backbenchers – a sign of how essential the system had become to family incomes – including in those middle England constituencies held by newly-elected Tory MPs.

Current challenges

When the Tory-led coalition came into power in 2010, George Osborne and his cabinet colleagues began to turn the clock back. For women, the 2010 budget was labelled the "worst since the creation of the welfare state".

The burden of the coalition's decision to rapidly accelerate deficit reduction ended up being borne most heavily by women.

Cuts to the top rate of tax helped more men while cuts to child benefit, maternity allowance, tax credits, public sector pay and pensions all hit women harder. So over the course of the coalition government more than 70 per cent of the revenue raised from direct tax and benefit changes came from women.

Once again, it was Labour women MPs who identified the inequalities. Research from the House of Commons library showed that the emergency budget introduced shortly after the general election cost women £5.8bn while men lost the much lesser figure of £2.2bn. The comprehensive spending review that autumn took a further £5.7bn from women, but less than half of this figure – £2.7bn – from men. The same research also showed that women were disproportionately affected by cuts to housing benefit, as 60 per cent of these cuts were in housing benefit paid to women.

The attacks on support to women did not end there. In 2016 the Resolution Foundation found that the Tories' flagship welfare reforms also hit women hardest, especially those in part-time work who are struggling to make ends meet. Under the much-hyped but deeply-flawed universal credit, second earners, who are so often women, will keep less of their earnings than they would under Labour's tax credits system. And there are disincentives in the system for part-time workers who want to increase their hours.

The cost-of-living squeeze under the Tories further undid much of the progress under Labour. Real wages in 2020 are still forecast to be below 2008 levels, which is the worst performance on record. Meanwhile rising inflation and £12bn of welfare cuts, including deep cuts due in April 2017, will continue to risk tipping women and their children into poverty.

It is no surprise therefore that recent research by the Joseph Rowntree Foundation has shown that poverty is rising again among the most vulnerable sections of our society. The number of households living below what the foundation considers an adequate income rose by a fifth – or 900,000 households – in three years. In addition, lack of childcare support for part-time workers has made it harder for working couples to make ends meet.

Worst of all, for the first time ever, most poor children have working parents: previously parental unemployment was the biggest risk factor for child poverty.

Against this backdrop, other challenges for women's employment remain.

The Institute for Public Policy Research has found that the UK continues to have a comparatively low maternal employment rate, and the employment rate of working age women overall is still around 10 percentage points lower than the 80 per cent figure for men. Wage inequality remains a problem, particularly for women returning to work after childbirth. The Institute for Fiscal Studies has shown that while the wage gap is around 10 per cent for men and women without children, the wage gap increases after child birth and, at the point where the first child is 12 years old, women's hourly wages are a third lower than men's.

So, where Labour thought that continued investment in tax credits and childcare was a price worth paying to get working families through the recession, the Tories thought quite the opposite. They cut spending in these vital areas in their doomed attempt to balance the budget in the lifetime of a single parliament. In the process they destroyed the support that had enabled families to weather the recessionary storms, and those hardest hit by their austerity economics were women.

Future campaigning

What then, should Labour women be doing now to champion economic equality?

First we need to restore the principle that women's equality matters for the economy and that the Treasury should take seriously the difference between the wallet and the purse. Focusing on overall household income as the Treasury now tries to do isn't good enough and ignores the importance of women's equality and women's independence. We need proper gender audits of policies for the future, and a tax and social security system designed to promote gender equality not to widen the divide.

Second we need universal childcare and a proper plan for social care – both should be treated as a central part of our economic infrastructure. Social care is becoming an economic issue on a similar scale to childcare, as growing numbers of older workers – especially women – are having to give up work to care for older relatives.

Third we need action to support women's equality in the changing economy. There are disproportionately few women employed in the growing number of relatively well paid jobs in technology and science: computer programmers are just one example. But women make up the majority of the swelling ranks of poorly paid care workers. Far more needs to be done on skills, training and reforming the way the economy works to make the most of new economic opportunities to support equality and growth. We also need to highlight the particular risks to women of a hard Brexit that results in wholesale deregulation of the UK labour market.

More should be done to support self-employment for women, and to protect the self-employed from exploitation in the new gig economy. Lack of access to finance and lack of childcare and maternity support disadvantage women starting up their own businesses. And whilst the new gig economy provides fresh opportunities for entry into the marketplace, we need fundamental changes both in the economy and in the welfare system to ensure it doesn't increase exploitation and leave women insecure and worse off.

There's been a growing trend in companies to contract for services rather than employ staff directly. The result is that the risks and insecurities once borne by employers now increasingly sit with the workers – formerly employees, now self-employed. These arrangements can hit women much harder, since they may offer flexibility, but do not normally allow for crucial maternity or parental leave. Labour women must be at the heart of the campaign for a better deal both in terms of employment rights and the welfare state to support workers in the new economy too.

In opposition, Labour women MPs will keep asking the difficult questions. For every budget we'll do a gender analysis to expose the impact on women, we'll make the case for childcare as infrastructure and we'll continue to push for much-needed reforms to social care – a crisis of our time which is hurting women hard. But the reality is, as our achievements laid out above show, that we can only change lives for the better from government. From 1997 to 2010 Labour made the country and the economy work better for women. Since 2010, the economic clock has been turned back. That's the difference Labour governments make – and it's the difference Labour women make.

If ever we forget why we are in politics, this pamphlet will serve as the best reminder.

2: THE NHS: WINNING THE CASE FOR INVESTMENT

Jacqui Smith and Liz Kendall MP

Labour created the NHS in 1948 – and in 1997 it expanded it. Now the challenge is to make the case for more investment in both health and social care, so that our NHS can underpin a growing economy.

> *'I pushed a box of tissues across the table to the elderly man who cried as he told me that he feared he would die before he got the heart operation his doctors told him he needed.'*
> **Jacqui Smith recalling a constituency surgery appointment soon after she was elected as MP for Redditch in 1997.**

NHS patients waited and suffered in 1997. There were more than 1 million people waiting for hospital treatment, and delays of up to 18 months before treatment were still common.

People working in today's NHS say that they haven't seen such tough times since before 1997. Times when NHS care was rationed by delays in treatment; when, if you could afford it, you paid to have your elderly relatives operated on in private hospitals and when satisfaction with NHS services was low. Today's Conservative government is reminding us what happens when funding and focus shift from providing timely access to health care. The NHS of all our great national institutions is particularly relevant to this publication. Women are more likely than men to come into contact with it through their caring responsibilities and comprise more than three-quarters of its workforce.

The last Labour government improved both the quantity and quality of NHS care. Before 1997, data about patient safety incidents in England was not comprehensive. There was little focus on learning from mistakes and too little research to ensure we delivered the best in our system. Access to health care and a healthy life depended too much on where people lived and how much they earned.

Whilst some mental health care had modernised, there was no systematic understanding about new ways to treat the many people with mental health problems. Stigma and prejudice against those suffering mental ill-health went unchallenged.

How did a Labour government rescue and reinvigorate the NHS which had been one of our greatest previous achievements in government? As we will see, it needed a considerable increase in investment – in staff, buildings and care. However it also needed reform to drive accountability to patients and a reinvigorated local leadership in the NHS and communities.

Labour in government: access and accountability

Waiting times for hospital care were a key issue in our 1997 election campaign – one of the five pledges on the famous card. On the doorstep, we talked to people about how we could cut NHS waiting lists by 100,000. This was achieved by 2000 – and we then went far further.

There was huge progress in speeding up access to hospital treatment, including for diagnostic tests and surgery, and improved access to GPs and other forms of primary care.

By 2010 most people waited no longer than 18 weeks for diagnostics and treatment – down from the 18 months when

How spending on health has slowed down

Figure 1: Average annual increase in government spending on health

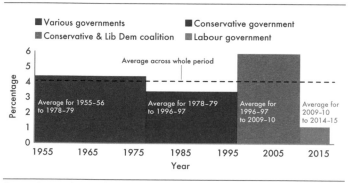

Source: Institute for Fiscal Studies

Labour came into government. There were half as many people on waiting lists and their waits were far shorter. The shift was in part brought about by substantial increases in the number of operations and diagnostic tests carried out. Between 1998/9 and 2007/8, the total number of procedures carried out in hospitals rose from 6.5 million to 8.6 million.

The focus wasn't only on hospital care. The NHS Plan in 2000 set a target for 2000 more GPs over five years. This ambition was easily met, with numbers increasing by 3,500 in that time. There were also more contacts with other primary care staff like nurses and pharmacists. These services were delivered in newly opened and renovated GP surgeries and increasingly in GP-led health centres.

The improvements could not have happened without the decision by a Labour government in the early 2000s to increase investment in healthcare to bring us up to the EU average. The difference between the record on health spending of the Labour government and the Conservative governments which went before and came after is stark, as shown in this diagram from the Institute for Fiscal Studies. The size of the respective columns translates into staff, equipment, buildings, access and quality – and the effects of the cuts post-2010 is the pain people are feeling now.

With more money came more accountability. The performance management of acute hospital services of the NHS was rigorous during the Labour years. Arguably stronger targets in community and mental health care could have improved access there too. Targets drive performance, but they are also an instrument of accountability. When Labour ministers translated the needs of people to be able to get their care quickly – regardless of their ability to pay – into targets for the system, they were enforcing the founding values of the NHS.

Too often the system of targets has been characterised by opponents inside and outside the NHS as being about bureaucratic interference with the professionals who know best. In fact, it was about accountability and delivering people's priorities more effectively. Despite people's fears at the time, more local accountability was also achieved through foundation trusts, accountable to members and with elected governors.

However there remains a problem at the local level where too often commissioning has neither properly engaged local people nor really driven providers to deliver the health services those people require. In too many cases, commissioning has tended just to administer national priorities through a burdensome local process or even acted as an additional regulator in the system.

The last few years have seen a weakening of the 'freedoms' of foundation trusts. Those providing NHS services are not looking outwards to the needs of their local communities and patients, but upwards with trepidation to central government diktats and a range of regulators.

Choice and involvement

Patient satisfaction as measured by the British Social Attitudes Survey was at its lowest point in 1997 and then grew throughout our period in government. Labour also introduced the biggest survey of patient experience in Europe.

From 2001 onwards, it also became a government priority to provide patients with choice over where they received non-urgent elective treatment.

We introduced personal budgets and direct payments in social care. These have given thousands of older and disabled people, and their families, greater control over their care and support.

In 2009, we extended personal budgets in a pilot scheme for people with long-term conditions like stroke, diabetes and mental health problems. The evidence shows personal health budgets improve people's quality of life, getting better results with the same amount of money. Where people had higher levels of need and larger personal budgets, their use of more expensive hospital services was actually reduced as they considered their options and made their choices.

Personal budgets can also be a powerful way of ensuring services are properly joined-up and keeping people well and living at home. Patients and families care more about getting the right help than which service or organisation provides it, and living day in, day out with a health condition means they often know best how to prevent it from getting worse.

Of course there are many situations where personal health budgets aren't suitable. In an emergency, few people are in a position to make choices about their treatment.

However for the growing number of people with long-term health conditions, personal budgets – backed up with the right information, advice and support – can help make sure people's views are taken into account much more than in the past. The shift in purchasing power from institution to individual works for everyone and provides choice for patients.

Choice has proved a controversial topic for some, but we would argue that the system does not yet deliver enough choice in a whole range of issues which affect the quality of care and patients' experience. Surveys have revealed several weaknesses, including limited progress in delivering greater choice of treatments, especially for mental health patients, and those reaching the end of their lives.

Quality and safety

The focus put on patient safety and quality was an important step forward by the Labour government. Reporting incidents and learning from them is key for today's successful health care providers even if there's more to be done to ensure that the system focuses on accountability and learning rather than blame and fault. Initiatives such as the National Patient Safety Agency helped to highlight the need for clinical quality. The focus on getting rid of hospital-acquired infections marked an end to the fatalistic view that there was not much that could be done, with instead an emphasis at national and trust level on safety.

More rigour was applied to establishing what worked best and should be delivered. With the National Institute for Clinical Excellence, the NHS made clear the criteria for the best medicines and treatments that people could expect across the system. After the NHS Plan in 2000, national service frameworks set out the types of treatment and care that the whole system should deliver. In mental health, for example, the development of new models of early intervention, crisis resolution, outreach and the introduction for the first time of talking therapies, transformed the quality of services.

Healthy lives

International comparisons of our health systems show the NHS performing extremely well on access and efficiency but less well on helping people to live healthy lives. It is a cliché, but nonetheless true, that we have developed an extremely successful national illness service, but have failed really to drive good health.

That's not to say we didn't make progress. Our teenage pregnancy strategy helped reduce conception rates among the under-18s to their lowest rates for more than 20 years. According to Cancer UK, Labour's ban on smoking in public places helped an estimated 400,000 people quit the habit.

As with many public health developments, critics criticised the smoking ban for being part of a 'nanny state' and dubbed the women ministers who stewarded it through 'nannies'. This is a gendered putdown to all those who considered that keeping people healthy was as important as trying to make them well again when they got ill. Perhaps it's also why governments have made poor progress in reducing obesity or diseases related to alcohol. No targets were set and no serious government action was taken on these – and still hasn't been.

The smoking ban was legislated and implemented by the Department of Health alone, but action on alcohol and obesity requires a cross-government approach. This has proved far more difficult to motivate and to lead inside government or outside.

Age discrimination was widespread in access to health services, especially to acute health care but this was only one aspect of health inequalities which Labour held to be completely unacceptable. Reducing health inequality became an explicit target for the first time and there was a focus on particularly deprived areas through initiatives such as health action zones.

Labour also took action to improve social care for older and disabled people. We pioneered new services to help older people stay living independently in their own homes, including through extra care housing and the Partnerships for Older People project. We championed more joined up NHS and social care services, introducing new care trusts for the first time. We introduced new rights for carers including the right to request flexible working, and improved information and advice for carers through the expert carers programme.

Closing health inequalities remained unfinished business. While life expectancy is growing across the population, it was and is still growing fastest for the better off, so the gap is widening. The barriers still haven't been properly broken down between the NHS and the other services that are needed to improve health standards in the most deprived communities. We need a wider approach that looks at economic and other social factors such as housing, and Labour was impatient in government to achieve this.

The future

But that was then. There were of course discordant voices. Not all of our reforms were welcomed, or went far enough, or were fully implemented or sufficiently funded. However, the commitment of Labour in government was absolute, and the progress in those years was from a much-loved but battered health care system to one that was delivering to the higher expectations and standards of the 21st century.

The Tories' onslaught on the NHS started immediately after the election. A divisive reorganisation, unprecedented in its scope and scale, drained an estimated £3bn away from frontline services, demoralised staff and diverted attention from the prime purpose of improving health outcomes. That was on top of the cuts in the growth in NHS spending shown above, so that budgets failed to keep pace with population increases, let alone rising costs or public expectations. There was an ideological onslaught on the notion of target-setting, seen as part of a Labour 'legacy of bureaucracy': until earlier this year when the King's Fund warned that after seven years of Tory and coalition government, a record 4 million people were waiting for operations. Two decades earlier Labour had committed to cut waiting lists – and delivered on that pledge.

In future, the biggest challenge for our health and care system is how we fund it. The NHS is partly the victim of its own success – people survive diseases which would have killed them in previous years, but they live longer with chronic diseases which need managing. We can do more for people when they are sick and they rightly expect that.

Labour must win the argument for more investment in both health and social care: these are not two separate services but are inextricably linked. We must also make the case that the NHS and social care don't just consume resources – they are vital to underpinning a growing economy. Helping people to stay fit and healthy for longer as our population ages, and providing decent support for carers, many of whom work as well as care for their loved ones, is as essential for our economy as it is for patients, users and families.

We have a unique asset in the NHS. There are few health systems globally in which there is potential access to so much data about the causes and cures of ill health and so much opportunity for trial and research. This government has bungled the issue of how we use patient data. We have a real opportunity to drive research, life sciences investment and jobs using the model of the NHS. Most importantly, this also provides the opportunity to find the personalised, effective treatments and technologies to put the NHS at the forefront of health care in the years to come.

In both health and social care, we need to finish the job of shifting choice and power to people. Giving service users and their families far more say and control should be at the heart of Labour's future approach to health and social care.

People's health often improves when they feel they are in control. We believe everyone, regardless of income, should have the same advantages as wealthy people who are able to choose the kind of care and support they need.

The people who know best how to join up their services and support are users and their families, because they don't see their needs through the prism of separate service silos. Developments in technology can help this to happen. Our best trusts already use technology to enable patients to access their care plans and records – and to share in decision-making. We are already developing apps to enable patients to organise their own follow-up treatment and ongoing care. This should be the norm for all who want it across health and care.

Users are often the strongest champions of prevention, because they are the ones who suffer the consequences if services fail to intervene early on.

And it is service users and their families who are frequently the toughest critics of inefficient services because they see the duplication and bureaucracy that wastes public money which would be better spent on improving their lives.

Making 'people power' a reality will require a profound change in the culture of our public services. It is not a £10 charge to see a GP which will ensure people take responsibility for their health, it's real information, choice and power.

In future, people can't be seen either as passive recipients of services, or as purely consumers. Instead, they must become genuine partners in co-designing and co-creating their care and support.

For this to happen, neither the old state-driven nor predominantly market-based approaches to public service reform will work because both can end up disempowering people.

Instead the new state will understand that people are genuine citizens with whom power and responsibility must be individually and collectively shared.

We should look back to 1945 with pride at what we created in the NHS, and to 1997 when we built on that legacy. But we also need to be able to look forward with optimism about what is still to come for this unique Labour achievement.

3: CHILDCARE: ENSURING A GOOD START TO LIFE

Caroline Flint MP and Sharon Hodgson MP

Intervening early in a child's life has a proven impact on poverty and inequality. The next generation of family policy must build on the achievements of the past to offer flexible and affordable childcare that's fit for the future.

Early years education was unfinished business from previous Labour governments and putting in place a high quality, comprehensive service was one of the great achievements of our last term in office.

In their two decades, the Thatcher and Major governments had failed to keep up with the changes in society – and the inequalities. When the Tories lost power, 3 million people had been on benefits for two years or more, one in five children had no working parent, and too many left school with no basic skills.

Poverty and inequality had increased sharply during the Conservative years. As a report by Lupton et al from the LSE has observed: "The proportion in poverty… remained almost twice as high in 1996/7 as it had been at the start of the 1960s. Inequality… was also at record levels."

Nursery education had been discussed by government since the 1960s. The Wilson government published the Plowden report which called for universal nursery education

In 1972, the then education secretary, Margaret Thatcher announced that: "Within 10 years nursery education should become available without charge to children of three or four whose parents wished them to have it." The main purpose was "to enable children to learn and not to provide a day-care service". Clearly, no connection was made between childcare or early years and the desire for women to work. In the end, the policy was never delivered.

By the time Mrs Thatcher became prime minister in 1979, the Tories had lost any desire to pursue early years education, and rejected childcare to support work. In 1980, social security minister George Young said: "In general, I do not accept that it is the state's job to provide day care to enable parents of young children to go out to work."

The Thatcher government eventually gave local councils the power, but no duty, to establish nursery classes. As a result, childcare and nursery education provision was patchy. In an era of substantial pressure on public services, as the Conservatives bore down on public spending, the development of municipal childcare provision, largely by Labour councils, occurred in spite of, not because of, government policy.

At the tail end of their 18 years in office, the Conservatives had few coherent policies aimed at tackling disadvantage or poverty. They failed to see patterns of intergenerational poverty. They knew that more women wanted to work, but failed to see the lack of affordable childcare as a barrier to women's aspirations, or as a mechanism to achieve equality in the workplace. By the mid-1990s, less than two thirds of women had entered the workforce, and growth had plateaued.

Tentative steps were taken at the last minute towards early years education. A pilot nursery voucher scheme was trialled in four local authority areas. In a sleight of hand, the government 'funded' the policy mainly by reducing the funds allocated to councils. The pilot scheme ended in April 1997 and the Major government left with public spending at a historic low and no national strategy for childcare.

Meanwhile the demand for childcare for working mothers had grown, with sustained campaigning by women's groups, trade unions, employers and childcare organisations for the state to play a greater role in the supply and affordability of childcare as well as other family-friendly policies. Alongside this was the rising number of lone parents unable to find and stay in work. The destiny for them and their children seemed to be a lifetime of poverty.

During the Conservative years there had been a blossoming of "municipal feminism" – a wave of policies in Labour councils influenced by the women's movement. Municipal childcare provision including workplace nurseries were a product of this thinking. The collective impact of Labour women was a sea change in our party's policy. Traditional opposition to a minimum wage had been replaced by support for it; we developed policy on paid maternity leave, equal pay, and childcare.

By 1986, Neil Kinnock, then party leader, was able to pledge: "We will make nursery education available for all three – and four-year-olds whose parents want this opportunity." And after the 1997 victory, New Labour was to go much further.

For the incoming Labour government here was the opportunity to tackle poverty and inequality in a profound way in response to the legacy of the preceding Tory years.

Early in its first term, the Labour government reaffirmed its commitment to women and children, especially the most disadvantaged. The 101 Labour women arriving in parliament included many young parents, but among the 400 all-party parliamentary groups, none existed on childcare. The new generation of Labour MPs, women and men, were to address the vacuum in this and other areas of social and economic policy.

Among a host of initiatives the Labour government established a social exclusion unit, a national childcare strategy, a cross-departmental ministerial group on family policy, a new deal for lone parents and a policy to reduce teenage pregnancy rates.

The mission was articulated in a report that laid the foundations for Labour's early years policy. Opportunity for All: Tackling Poverty and Social Exclusion said in its introduction: "Our aim is to end the injustice which holds people back and prevents them from making the most of themselves. That means making sure that all children, whatever their background and wherever they live, get a first-class education... Put simply, our goal is to end child poverty in 20 years."

From its first days, the contrast between Labour's commitment and the neglect of the Major years was obvious.

The ad-hoc voucher policy was replaced by an entitlement to a fully-funded part-time place in nursery education for every four-year-old. By funding the new offer across a range of childcare settings both public, private and charitable, the government underpinned a new approach.

The goals for early years policy were threefold:
- Improving the education and the outcomes for children from disadvantaged backgrounds.
- Removing the barriers to women gaining work or training to boost the UK labour force.
- Reducing child poverty.

The power of local authorities to provide pre-school education was replaced with a duty to provide sufficient places, if not within their schools, then with partners.

Unlike the previous administration, the Labour government built the extra funding for early years into a dedicated schools grant and also required the inequalities in funding between different types of providers to be ended by 2010/11.

Looking at evidence from the Clinton administration in the United States, Labour created Sure Start – an innovation in family policy which brought together health, education and family support with childcare – to intervene early in a child's life and support mother and child together. At a Sure Start centre a child could be in a nursery, while mum was attending parenting or literacy classes in the same building. With outreach and easy access to related services, this was family intervention at community level. Starting with "trailblazer" pilots in 1998, by 2010, Labour established 3,500 Sure Start children's centres.

The new early years guarantee for four-year-olds, was the first of many steps to establishing a comprehensive early years approach. It provided a national standard offer of a free place – a morning or afternoon session every day, totalling 12.5 hours, for 33 weeks. By 2004, the service was extended to cater all three-years-olds; and by 2006, the entitlement was upped to 15 hours for 38 weeks. By 2009, 10 to 15 hours of early education was also offered to the 25 per cent most disadvantaged two-year-olds.

To lead the national childcare strategy, Margaret Hodge MP was appointed as the first minister for children, a post that continues to this day.

By 2010, Labour had shifted the centre of gravity such that all parties were competing with an early education offer, which following the election, led to Labour's proposal for 15 hours of free childcare being rolled out, which the Tories took credit for.

At the 2015 general election, Labour offered 25 hours free childcare to working parents, fully-costed. The Tories pledged 30 hours to an estimated 600,000 households, only to tighten the criteria reducing the numbers to 390,000, and so the cost. Nearly two years on from this manifesto pledge, the Tories are now not delivering this promise and instead creating uncertainty in the early years system.

Labour had modernised and feminised children and family policy. Twenty years ago, childcare and family policy would never have been central campaign policies for the two main parties; the fact that they are now is down to Labour.

Childcare and equality

The 1997 Labour government's package of childcare and tax credits freed more women to go to work, and by 2002 the proportion of women at work had risen to a record 69.5 per cent. Crucial to this was the growth of private day nurseries.

The establishment of the early years foundation stage led to a pre-school curriculum to standardise early years education. This curriculum drove up the quality of pre-school provision and increased professionalism, in a sector that had been viewed by some as low-skilled work.

As government funding of early years education and tax credits for childcare operated across public and private sectors, both could deliver the curriculum. The private sector could develop its staff whilst offering both care and early learning for the children of working parents.

The introduction of childcare tax credits, alongside a new deal for lone parents, changed the relationship with parents who were largely on benefits, with few skills. While their children learned social skills, women were gaining work-related skills.

Breakfast clubs were established, starting in the most deprived neighbourhoods. The logic was simple – a well-fed child would learn better.

Ministers realised that the school day did not match the working day; and the concept of 8am–6pm schools was developed through the extended schools programme. For many parents this could provide the quality wrap-around childcare for school age children, once "latch-key kids".

Sadly, the programme was never fully embedded. The in-coming coalition government paid lip service to the policy, removing the core element of childcare provision in primary schools, scrapping the ring-fenced budget and incorporating the funding into the dedicated schools grant which was then cut by the Tories.

The use of childcare tax credits to meet the bulk of child-care costs to support parents in employment reinforced Labour's belief in welfare to work. For us work was the key to addressing poverty. "Work is the most important route out of low income," stated Opportunity for All. For Labour, childcare tax credits were a hand-up, not a handout. Government would 'help people to help themselves'.

These policies were not cheap, but government research showed that every extra woman entering the workforce was saving society £20,000 a year.

By 2010, the proportion of lone parents in the workforce was at a record high. Labour's childcare and early years poli-cies were central to this social change. Active welfare to work policies could not have worked without the childcare compo-nent, something that previous Tory governments had failed to grasp, but no government will ever lose sight of again.

Changing outcomes

Labour changed the landscape of early years services and support for families.

It provided a universal entitlement to early years educa-tion, a childcare infrastructure, and a parental expectation that was impossible to reverse. In doing so, it developed both a curriculum for pre-school education and a trained workforce for delivering it. The impact was dramatic. In 1994 only five per cent of under fives were in nursery schooling. By 2010 the figure had soared to 94 per cent of three and four-year-olds. Expansion of childcare places was equally dramatic, peaking at 838,000 in 2008, up 36-fold from its 1997 level.

The national childcare strategy required substantial ongoing investment: it was never an inexpensive policy. This was forthcoming from Labour, and by 2006, the Institute for Fiscal Studies noted that 'the UK had the second highest level of spending per pupil in the pre-primary sector amongst the 26 OECD countries'. In 2010 the IFS also noted that real increases in spending on the under 5s in England rose by 6.1 per cent a year for every full year of the Labour government.

As the Lupton/LSE research concluded: 'For young children, employment rates among lone parents improved... Child poverty fell from 27 per cent in 1996/7 to 17.5 per cent in 2010/11.'

One could argue that such trends could have happened naturally, but the previous 18 years of failed trickle-down showed that an active government strategy was decisive. We would argue that childcare, early years and Sure Start were crucial to achieving those outcomes.

The government's programme to eradicate child poverty and boost women's role in society was fuelled by a 60 per cent increase in public spending over the lifetime of the government; and 78 per cent increase in education spending. Half of the increase in the social security budget went to children, and in-work benefits were raised in line with earnings.

As one element of a huge government agenda, it has stood the test of time. The true test of social policy changes is whether they leave a legacy, not least whether subsequent governments adopt rather than repeal, the heart of the policy.

Early years education is now embedded in our school and childcare system. Childcare tax credits, and their successor under universal credit, underpinning childcare costs, have survived. Sure Start has been undermined by the coalition and Tory governments but children centres are still hanging on, though with only a shadow of their previous reach and capacity. Nearly 800 centres have closed since 2010.

The past seven years have seen a stalling and fragmentation, a withering of initiative as a result of lack of government ambition reinforced by the constraints on spending after the global economic crash.

Labour's challenge remains to refine and extend this agenda to fulfil the social purpose we identified in 1997 of combatting poverty and inequality and improving the life chances of every child.

Childcare and family-friendly policies must respond to new pressures in a labour market that for many is more insecure than it was 20 years ago. Paid paternity leave, the right to request flexible hours and the move to shared parental leave all play their part in creating a more equal and balanced role between parents, although in reality, women still juggle the lion's share of parental and domestic duties.

As public policy makers focus on creating a modern industrial strategy where does childcare provision sit? Should it be an infrastructure priority along with broadband, housing and transport? Will future skills shortages post-Brexit require more women to enter the jobs market?

Whilst the amount of support to families with childcare costs has increased, for many it is still too expensive and bureaucratic. Many childcare providers are being asked by the state to double the hours of nursery education without being fully funded. The danger of this development is that private nurseries risk closure or parents face greater costs. This could result in some nurseries refusing to take children for the free 30 hours, resulting in a divisive two-tier nursery system.

In the 21st century it must be the ambition of a future Labour Britain to provide a universal entitlement to childcare that is simpler, more flexible and affordable.

4: OLDER WOMEN: A COMMITMENT
TO LIFELONG EQUALITY

Fiona Mactaggart MP and Anne Begg

Labour made great strides in tackling poverty among pensioners – and among older women in particular. But big challenges remain. Older women are still too often absent from the public policy debate. We need to celebrate their contribution to our society, workplaces, families and neighbourhoods.

Labour's pension challenge in 1997 was to end the poverty in which almost half of all pensioners then lived. Women pensioners were most likely to be poor. The state pension system wasn't designed with them in mind, and the result was that 1.5 million women pensioners found themselves in poverty after a lifetime of working and caring.

The choice confronting the new government was whether to reform the pension system to end pensioner poverty or to succumb to the clamour from many pensioner groups for a universal increase in the basic state pension, the value of which had eroded during the Tory years.

Labour's achievement was to deliver for poor pensioners – to cut by more than two-thirds the proportion of those living in absolute poverty. By 2010 women pensioners were less likely than the rest of the population to be living in poverty – a complete reversal from the position inherited from the Tories.

Social and economic factors combine to make women pensioners vulnerable to poverty. Women live longer, often outliving their partners, and so face a higher risk of being ill or disabled in very old age. In 1997 when Labour was elected, most older women had spent long periods out of formal work, caring for children or other family members. Many had given up jobs when their children were born, and were financially dependent on their spouses. A disproportionate number of the poorest women pensioners were aged over 75.

But the 1960s and 1970s saw the wider availability of reliable birth control which enabled women to manage their fertility, to remain in the labour market or to commit to the extended education required by professional careers. By 1997 the women who had benefited from these changes were around 50 years old. Their needs and expectations in retirement were different from their older sisters for whom the most pressing problem was an easing of the poverty in which they lived.

Many women were caught in a poverty trap because the pensions system was based on an outmoded model of family and society that undervalued their paid employment and placed no value on their caring role.

- Most women had been unable during their working years to build up the 39 years of national insurance contributions required to qualify for a full pension.
- Many women had opted for the 'married women's stamp' a reduced contribution that did not qualify them for a full pension.
- Few women had been able to contribute to the state earnings related pension scheme which topped up the basic pension.
- Trapped in part-time, informal or low-paid jobs, few women had savings or the occupational pensions that used to be the bedrock for financial well-being in retirement.

As a result, many women pensioners were dependent on means-tested income support as their main source of income or as a top-up. In 1997, when the state pension for a single person was £62.45 a week, those on income support had a total weekly income of just £68.80.

What Labour achieved in government

1. Increasing pensioner incomes

It was the introduction of pension credit that made the difference, reducing the number of pensioners living in absolute poverty from 45 per cent in 1997 to 14 per cent by the time Labour left office. It particularly benefited women for whom an increase in the state pension would have done little to help: most women pensioners didn't qualify for a full state pension. Despite early difficulties, pension credit has become well established and popular.

There were two parts to pension credit. The first was the minimum income guarantee. It did not depend on a record of national insurance contributions, but instead ensured that pensioners were guaranteed a minimum weekly income whatever its source. So by 2001, while the basic state pension for a single pensioner was £72.50 a week, the minimum income guarantee, thanks to pension credit, ensured no pensioner received less than £92.15 a week. By the time Labour left office the minimum income guarantee had increased a single pensioner's income from £68.80 to £132.60. For a couple it had increased from £106.80 to £202.40. This represented a near doubling of incomes for these – the poorest – pensioners.

The second part of the pension credit was savings credit. This was designed to make sure that people who had an income just above the minimum level also benefited from the new system and were better off than those with no savings or second pension. However, the savings credit was poorly understood and the calculations were complex so it wasn't easy for people to work out their entitlement. In addition, those who benefited were generally people who hadn't previously qualified for 'benefits' and were often reluctant to claim.

The decision to concentrate on the poorest pensioners before restoring the value of the basic state pension was not without controversy. Especially vocal were pensioner groups, many of them run by those who qualified for the state pension and some form of second pension. They felt aggrieved that their pension was not increasing, and their frustration was compounded by the 75p a week pension increase announced in 1999. This was in line with the rise in inflation – but was a move that is still used to discredit all the work done to increase pensioners' income while Labour was in government.

2. Providing quality of life benefits
Quality of life benefits also tackled the poverty of older women. Particularly notable was the introduction of the winter fuel payment, which by 2010 stood at £250 for the over-60s and £400 for the over-80s. In 1999, free TV licences were introduced for the over-75s. Two years later, Labour introduced a concessionary travel scheme, which started with half-price bus fares and was gradually extended over the following seven years. This disproportionately benefited women: in 1997 only 15 per cent of women over 60 were drivers and women are still significantly more likely than men to use public transport.

3. Supporting carers
One of the breakthroughs for women was the recognition Labour gave to the role we play as carers, including in our

later years. A listening exercise by the ministers for women, new positions created in 1997, showed that balancing work and family life was the top priority for women. Responding to this priority helped to drive the childcare strategy, parental leave and maternity pay changes. And importantly, it made a big difference for women in middle and older age who cared for grandchildren and older or disabled relatives. As carers, they had already acquired some rights through Labour MP Malcolm Wicks' private members' bill of 1995. Major improvements were introduced by the Labour government in 2007 with weekly carers credits and two years later people caring for grandchildren or other family members were able to gain national insurance credits.

4. Legislating against age and gender inequality

Labour is the party with equality at the heart of its mission, and older women were the beneficiaries of some of our most progressive legislation. Early on, following an initiative by backbench Labour MP Linda Perham, age discrimination in job advertising was banned by a code of practice and job centres were stopped from offering jobs with an upper age limit.

Women were the biggest winners from Labour's landmark minimum wage legislation. It especially helped older women who still face a wider gender pay gap than their younger sisters.

The 2010 Equalities Act, one of the last and most radical pieces of legislation of the Labour government, included a mechanism to recognise the way age and gender could combine to compound inequality. Yet the coalition government decided not to proceed with this section of the act.

Another groundbreaking section of the act, which provides for pay audits, only came into effect this year. It should provide the evidence that older women face a particularly wide pay gap and pave the way for further action.

Older women post 2010: the WASPI women

There were setbacks when Labour left office. The biggest losers under the coalition's austerity programme were women in low-paid public sector jobs, and especially older women. Unemployment among women aged 50 to 64 increased by 41 per cent between 2010 and 2013. Many turned to self-employment and it is notable that most of those who are newly self-employed are aged over 55 and two-thirds of them are women. Yet they still earn only half as much as their male counterparts.

The coalition government boasted that women would be particular beneficiaries of the new flat rate state pension introduced in the 2014 Pensions Act. However, to make it affordable, the act contained two stings in the tail for women, provisions that deprived one group of their right to a state pension – the Women Against State Pension Inequality, or WASPI.

The first was the decision by the coalition to increase the number of years people had to work to get a state pension. Labour's 2007 Act had reduced this to 30 years. The coalition increased it to 35 years. This left in the lurch a group of people who had stopped work assuming they had already made the 30 years of national insurance contributions they needed to qualify for a full state pension.

The second provision – which had an even more disastrous impact – was the increase in the state pension age for both men and women to 66 between 2018 and 2020. This decision cut across existing policy to equalise men and women's pension age over time. The WASPI women rightly feel incensed at the way they've been treated. Their vociferous campaign has been strongly supported by Labour women MPs, including Debbie Abrahams, shadow work and pensions secretary. Labour's proposal to extend pension credit to this group would have gone a long way to ease the pressures on this group of women.

But the Tories refused to act. As a result, many WASPI women who found themselves out of work in their late 50s and have been unable to get jobs have become dependent on out of work benefits or a working spouse. Others who had taken early retirement in the expectation of receiving their state pension have been left waiting another two years for it. They weren't to know when they made the decision to retire that the law would change at such short notice.

There is an immediate need for the benefits system to recognise the dire financial straits some of these women are in. Some may qualify for a disability benefit such as employment and support allowance but these too have been cut. For some women then it feels like a return to the 1950s when wives were dependent on their husbands for their spending money.

The future challenge for older women

Social and economic changes continue to confront older women with new challenges. To explore these, Labour in opposition established the Older Women's Commission which was chaired by Harriet Harman, and included a diverse range of older women from the public and private sectors. The commission held hearings with groups of women around the country, focusing on three main issues:

● Women and work
● Caring responsibilities
● The invisibility of older women in public life

Some of the commission's proposals, such as allowing women to choose to share maternity leave with their mothers, rather than their spouses, led to robust debates about letting partners off the hook. The commission avoided dealing with short-term pension problems, largely because of anxiety in the party hierarchy about making unfunded spending commitments in the run-up to the crucial 2015 general election. But generally the commission's conclusions were welcomed, although regrettably nothing was done by the party to feature them in our election offer.

More radically, the commission proposed measures that would support the long-term financial security of older women. It highlighted the continuing compound age and gender discrimination that older women face in the labour market, and argued for positive action to stop employer discrimination. It called for action over the changes to the state pension age due to take place before 2020, and further, recommended that the next Labour government should pledge to safeguard rules around the state pension age to provide certainty for people planning their retirement.

The commission helped to highlight previously neglected areas of gender discrimination. One example was the way in which women disappear from view as they get older, are less likely to appear in the media as interviewers or experts, or to be visible participants in public or corporate life. Older men are credited with gravitas, older women become invisible. Labour in government should establish a similar commission to ensure that it tackles the historic inequalities experienced by older women, and is sensitive to the emerging issues that affect their lives.

One of the pressing injustices to which older women may hold the key are the intergenerational inequalities that leave younger people poorer and often homeless. The current generation of older people are often asset-rich even if cash-poor, and that asset is often housing. Britain lags behind many other countries in developing suitable housing to help older people to give up the homes where they have brought up a family and establish themselves in a smaller, more manageable space. As secure tenancies in social housing are being ended, there is an incentive for people to stay put there too. It's time for a careful look at how better to support older people wanting to downsize. This particularly affects women who are more likely to outlive their partners and be alone in old age. We need incentives in the tax and benefit system to enable women to make choices that are right for them and address and help ease the intergenerational housing divide.

The biggest challenge though is to recognise and celebrate the potential of older women. So often they are the glue which keeps neighbourhoods working, by taking on voluntary roles, or workplaces running smoothly by mentoring younger workers. Their experience should be valued in the public policy debate which for too long has been dominated by men. Hard work by feminists in parliament and wider society has changed some of the stereotypes. But while it is not acceptable to display pictures of naked women in the workplace or to sexually harass colleagues, older women are still the butt of jibes about the menopause and mothers-in-law. The better workplace rights, including maternity leave and equal pay we have won for younger women are not yet replicated in the lives of their mothers and grandmothers who need flexible work to care for ill husbands or frail parents.

Britain is getting older and for our society to work effectively we need to use the talents of older members of society. That means valuing them at work and making employment flexible enough to allow them to care for their families. It means making sure that women over 50 don't disappear, from our television screens, boardrooms and workplaces. It means making sure they have a predictable income as they get older and that they have choices so that they can share any wealth they have acquired with their children and grandchildren. It means supporting them as carers and helping them to remain independent for as long as possible. Equality must be lifelong.

5: GETTING THERE:
PART ONE: THE 1997 INTAKE

Laura Moffatt

For the women MPs elected in 1997, serving in the new intake felt like being part of a revolution. It was a time of optimism, landmark legislation and a sense of solidarity.

In the early hours of Friday 2 May 1997 as the general election count concluded, I left one of the most respected professions – NHS nurse – and became an MP. Like all of the Labour women members elected that day, I was full of hope and a sense of purpose that the Labour government could make a difference. And despite some arguing we were just "Blair's Babes", we really did work hard to change our constituents' lives for the better.

Many years of working in the NHS as a registered nurse served me well. The all-night sittings we endured in the early days were easy for me having been on a busy ward on night duty just a few weeks previously. I used to jump up when the division bell rang out in the early hours as I momentarily thought it was a patient pressing their call bell.

I wanted to become an effective member of parliament and wanted to use the experience of my nursing background to benefit my constituents. As it happened, my NHS experience was later to be sorely tested in a major reorganisation of the NHS services used by my constituents. They too would sometimes get my new role a little muddled up with my old one. At an early constituency advice surgery a lovely gentleman came tell me about his experience in the NHS and took his trousers down to show me his hernia repair scar.

But I also wanted to work on other issues as well, and didn't want to become a 'one trick' MP. It was vital to me to learn quickly how to make the House of Commons work for me and the people of Crawley, and also to work on a wider range of policies.

So I joined the defence select committee alongside my Labour colleague and friend Dari Taylor MP. We were the first two women to serve on this committee and we brought a new perspective to issues like housing for armed forces families, domestic violence within the services and the better emergency care for injured service personnel. The committee reports on these subjects stand the test of time and I am proud to have contributed to getting better care for our armed forces.

Not that we concentrated on so-called women's issues. That was not and should not have been an option. We also took part in the inquiry into Britain's nuclear deterrent and the Chinook helicopter crash on the Mull of Kintyre. But changing the emphasis of the committee made it more effective and more equal in the subjects it looked at if not fully in its gender make-up.

There were so many newly elected Labour women MPs in 1997 and we needed each other. There were many acts of kindness and support. If a woman MP had picked her way through the complicated private members' bill process, her experiences would be shared to help others. Looking out for members struggling with a new job and living away from home and children was very much part of the lifestyle in the early days.

That momentous election changed the face of politics by challenging the look and feel of the House of Commons. New women MPs from very many backgrounds – journalists, finance officers, nurses, teachers, housing officials and more – brought new thinking to work alongside more experienced members. It was an optimistic time to join the Commons, especially when we were able to vote through the landmark Labour legislation: the minimum wage, more childcare, tax credits. But our investment in the NHS will remain our greatest achievement in my view.

I happily absorbed the long hours and limited time off to be part of what felt like a revolution. As that first term progressed, the Labour women MPs grew in confidence. Far from being fodder for the Labour frontbench we pursued issues of great importance to us and our constituents. Of course, we supported our Labour government on the floor of the House of Commons. Of course, we congratulated ministers as the Labour manifesto was enacted.

I honestly thought I would be elected for one term only so was delighted to be re-elected in 2002. The momentum was still with us, but we were to face the biggest challenge of the 1997–2010 Labour government with the Iraq war. The debates were robust and difficult. Each one of us were aware of the consequence of our vote and what we was asking others to do on our behalf. Many of us were in a very dark place and grappled with our consciences and many of us struggle to this day.

MPs deal with the big national issues alongside focusing on policies in which they have special interest and expertise. At the same time, they have to serve their constituents with personal and constituency problems. Those of us elected in 1997 were encouraged to work hard, to fight for every vote and keep on campaigning after the election.

One of my special interests was healthcare, and in partnership with a coalition of nursing and health organisations, I developed a piece of legislation – a private members' bill – to reduce needlestick injuries to health and care workers. These injuries can have devastating health implications and cause huge stress to people waiting to see if they've contracted bloodborne diseases.

By chance I had to present the bill on the floor of the House of Commons in the electrified 10 minutes between Tony Blair's prime minister's questions and the start of the first debate on Iraq. So the green benches were packed. My private members' bill stood no chance of becoming law but I had a huge audience and got so much publicity that it kick-started the move to use safe needles. And I now see the results of this every working day.

In 2010 I decided to retire from the House of Commons and return to nursing. I wanted to end my working life as it began, as a nurse.

So now I'm back on the front line in the NHS seeing the effect of those Labour years. For example I see the Mental Capacity Act used each day to secure the rights of people using our mental health services. It fills me with pride as just one of the massive tranche of laws brought in by the Labour government.

In both nursing and as a member of parliament I have shed tears of pain and rage, been driven mad with frustration and been delighted with successes both small and large. Both jobs have more in common than I could have believed and complement each other every day. It was a huge privilege to serve the people of Crawley from 1997 until 2010. I see Labour women MPs working today just as hard to bring their life experience to bear to benefit both their constituents and the wider UK public.

We should reflect and celebrate the achievements of Labour women MPs over the last 20 years be they in power or opposition. Without them parliament would be much the poorer.

Paula Sherriff MP

Parliament today is a very different place from how it was even 20 years ago. But while there has been progress, there are still barriers to overcome – and a final glass ceiling to smash.

L abour women down the decades who have become MPs have paved the way for others to follow in their footsteps. But it's still not an easy task. My own background did not perhaps make me the most obvious candidate. I did not have years of experience in politics – when I was selected to run for Dewsbury and Mirfield, I had been a local councillor for under two years. Neither did I have the public school or university background shared by so many candidates. According to the Sutton Trust, almost a third of parliamentary candidates in 2015 were privately educated, compared with just 7 per cent of the UK population in general, while 19 per cent were Oxbridge graduates and 55 per cent had attended Russell Group universities.

Nor was I full of confidence. Although I had been a shop steward for years and so had plenty of experience representing people, I was surprised and delighted to be selected. It was only on the way home after the selection meeting that I realised what a huge step this was.

All-women shortlists have not been without controversy, but they have made a difference in getting women selected, and then elected. I was one of those selected from an all-women shortlist and the selection process had been quite a divisive one, with some party members opposed. But after it was over the constituency came together quickly.

Being selected is of course only the first stage of a long campaign. Candidates without significant personal resources have to juggle their day jobs with campaigning. The campaign itself demands resilience, so you have to believe in yourself. You need to have the conviction that you can win – and you also need some good friends so that you can go and cry on their shoulders when you have a bad day campaigning. You need some good local issues you can campaign on. I campaigned on the cuts affecting Dewsbury hospital. My dad was a cancer survivor, so campaigning for the hospital was a labour of love. Most of all you need to be true to yourself, because if you're not you soon get caught out.

Once you are an MP, life changes again. Arriving in Westminster, the deference I encountered surprised and amused me. I had hardly ever been to London before, and had only visited parliament twice in my whole life. Other new MPs talked about how they had been special advisers and which universities they had been to, and about complex mechanisms of the legislative process. I had been working in healthcare, and hadn't been to university, and felt totally out of place.

But speaking to colleagues, I realised that I had spent 22 years working in the police and criminal justice system and for the NHS and had resolved problems that others would not find easy. They would not have been able to deal with some of the things I had handled. It was just like starting any new role – you learn on the job.

Becoming an MP is immediately immersive. There is no probationary period to get to grips with the challenges you may face. I had been an MP for just five weeks when a former constituent blew himself up with a suicide bomb in Syria. I put out a statement and then I got a series of awful messages through email, facebook and twitter. One was a credible death threat, which I reported to the police who arrested the man.

The following summer, Jo Cox MP was horribly murdered. Her constituency of Batley and Spen borders on mine and we had worked closely on many issues that affect both areas, including having been vocal in opposing right wing extremists and hate crimes. Jo was senselessly taken from us. Having been part of the same intake of MPs in 2015 and representing a neighbouring constituency, I knew her as a tireless and passionate MP who embraced the difficult issues. Her death was horrific and we are all still devastated by it. The memory of her remains a strong force in the community and with everyone who knew her.

Right from the start, I made it my first priority to be a good constituency MP. Alongside my community campaigning, I am motivated by the three big issues that politicised me: trade unionism, feminism and the NHS.

I'm proud of my successful campaign to scrap VAT on sanitary products or the 'tampon tax'. It got parliament talking about something that had been a taboo. I've had emails from women all round the world saying, "Thanks for allowing us to talk about periods."

I've also set up an all-party parliamentary group on women's health. We have had a hearing on cervical smears, as the take-up of these is the lowest it has been for 13 years. We are holding hearings on endometriosis and fibroids, and are planning a campaign on the menopause, to get it recognised in legislation. That's another area which isn't talked about in politics. We want to get exclusion zones around abortion clinics because women can still be harassed on their way into them.

Another issue that I'm campaigning on is for an end to sexist surcharges, forcing up the price of products that are marketed to women. Razors designed for women, for example, and so made in pink, are often more expensive than razors marketed for men.

So have things moved on for women MPs from the parliament our predecessors encountered? Despite the greater number of women MPs, there is still a fair amount of sexism in parliament. Some male Tory MPs say outrageous things, shout down female MPs and then seem to think that if they say sorry it is all OK. Or they pass it off as a joke. Or they try to patronise us, like David Cameron's "Calm down dear." We need to be stronger in objecting to it more often, and calling it out for what it is.

The lack of women MPs in other parties is a visible problem. When we sit on the Labour benches – where 45 per cent of MPs are women – and look across at the Tory benches, sometimes there are no women MPs sitting there at all.

Having all-women shortlists has been important and has made a real difference to our parliamentary party, but of course we are still struggling to smash the final glass ceiling and have a woman elected as Labour leader and prime minister.

And just as the women MPs elected in the past paved the way for the parliament we see today, so we look forward to the politicians of the future making a difference. Recently I went to do a school assembly, and afterwards a young girl came up to talk to me. She said she had never imagined that she would meet me and burst into tears. I told her: "Never let anyone tell you that you can't reach for the stars."

6: THE WORLD OF WORK:
PART ONE: THE WORKING WOMAN'S VOICE

Frances O'Grady

Despite significant progress for women at work, they are still more likely to be paid less, trained less and promoted less than their male colleagues. Add in the changing labour market and the spectre of fewer employment rights post-Brexit and it's clear that the time is right for a new deal for women workers.

The trade union movement has a long and proud history of representing – and winning for – women workers. From the chainmakers of Cradley Heath and the Bryant & May match workers through to the sewing machinists at Ford in Dagenham, trade union women have organised, bargained and campaigned for a fairer, more equal future for ourselves and our daughters. Now begins another chapter in that collective story.

A record number of women are now in work, the result of decades of profound economic and social change. The decline of manufacturing, the growth of services, new ways of organising work itself all underpinned the increasing feminisation of our labour market. Despite this, women remain second-class citizens in the workplace – more likely to be in low-paid jobs and sectors, more likely to be discriminated against, more likely to lose out when it comes to progression. Putting right these wrongs is a central priority for trade unions, just as it is for Labour.

Our movement has already won significant progress for women at work, not least during the 13 years of Labour government after 1997. The achievements of that period are worth recounting, even now: a minimum wage that disproportionately benefited women; huge investment in public services and public sector jobs; a nationwide network of Sure Start centres; important new rights at work and fairness for vulnerable workers through the regulation of gangmasters.

But we did not go far enough. Even after three terms of Labour government, our labour market remained one of the least regulated anywhere in the OECD; the gender pay gap remained stubbornly high; the glass ceiling prevented women from achieving their true potential; many thousands of public sector women had been outsourced with their jobs into the private sector; and our childcare was still amongst the most expensive in the world. More fundamentally, genuine flexibility in the workplace – giving real choice to both women and men – remained elusive.

Growing income inequality was a key driver of the financial crisis, the long recession it caused, and the persistent squeeze in living standards with women on the frontline. The coalition government's ideological choice to shrink the state by imposing years of austerity cast a long shadow. Almost 1 million public sector jobs were axed, the majority held by women. Cuts to health, education and council services were felt most keenly by women. And the evidence shows that radical 'reforms' to the welfare system hit women harder than men.

The election of a majority Conservative government in May 2015 means that this agenda is here to stay for some time. Its Trade Union Act was designed to make it harder to fight back, especially for women because they are more likely to work in public services where new voting thresholds apply. The Trades Union Congress and unions ran a vigorous campaign against the reforms, stripping the original trade union bill of some its most pernicious provisions. Throughout, our messaging stressed the impact on women; indeed our campaign posters featured three women who had recently taken strike action as a last resort – a midwife, a cinema worker and a firefighter.

As unions get to grips with a cold political climate, we must also address a new set of challenges facing women at work. Perhaps most dramatically, we face a revolution in the workplace whose speed and scale is possibly unprecedented. If the benefits were shared fairly, automation, algorithms and new technology could help enrich work but instead they look set to destroy jobs. Similarly, too often the rise of the gig economy risks undermining steady jobs and entrenching decidedly very old-fashioned forms of casualisation. Studies show that women account for the majority of workers on zero-hours contracts, in temporary work or employed by an agency. Meanwhile, women account for just one in four of the workforce in the new digital jobs.

The second challenge before us is facing down the systemic discrimination built into so much of the contemporary labour market. Women are still paid less, promoted less and trained less than their male colleagues – a national scandal in a modern industrial democracy. Occupational segregation is one of the defining contours of our workplace landscape, with women overwhelmingly concentrated in the low-paid 'five Cs': caring, catering, cashiering, cleaning and clerical. Opportunities to work part-time or flexibly in better paying parts of the economy remain painfully thin. And regardless of where they work, pregnant women and mothers returning to work receive a particularly raw deal: well over 50,000 women are forced out of their jobs each year, and one in five new mothers experiences harassment. Yet the introduction of fees for tribunal has made it even harder for women to challenge such discrimination. Since the £1,300 tribunal charge was introduced, we have seen a sharp drop-off in the number of discrimination claims – and not because we've seen a sharp fall in discrimination.

The third key challenge facing women – indeed all working people – is Brexit. Although the government says it is not seeking to repeal popular rights at work, such as paid holidays, that emanate from the European Union, the real danger is that workers in Britain will begin to fall behind our friends elsewhere. The TUC will be lobbying hard for a positive, progressive deal with the EU that safeguards jobs, investment and rights. The alternative – the UK as a cheap labour, offshore tax haven dependent on the largesse of trade deals with the Trump administration – does not bear thinking about.

So this is a critical time for working women in the UK. Trade unions face a uniquely challenging set of circumstances at a time when our legal rights have been severely curtailed. And when it comes to the complex set of issues facing women at work, there is no silver bullet. The solutions lie in a mix of policy, regulation and legislation; stronger trade unions and more collective bargaining; a genuine living wage and modern wages councils setting higher pay rates; investment in our public services; and – as the Women's Budget Group has rightly argued – investment in our social infrastructure such as social care and childcare.

For our part, the TUC will be calling for a new deal for working women. And that demands a radical change in mindset, so we deliver genuine flexibility for all at work, men as well as women. We urgently require a better supply of well-paid, part-time work at all organisational levels. We need decent, affordable childcare accessible to everyone. And we need fairness for the care workforce too. It cannot be right that care workers in Australia earn the average wage, yet here in the UK they earn significantly less than half.

More broadly, we've got to challenge the misrepresentation of the new, precarious world of work as 'flexible', when all the flexibility – indeed all the power – resides with the employer. Just as significantly, we must challenge the deeply entrenched social norm that depicts men as the primary breadwinner and women as the primary carer. We also need to challenge the silence over the fact that half of women experience sexual harassment and the way in which a boss can tell women how high their heels should be. The way we think about work – who does what and how it is rewarded – needs to change. Women workers are wealth creators too and want a voice all the way to the top.

All of this poses a challenge for the trade union movement too. With a membership now comprising women and men 50:50, we may be significantly less pale, male and stale than a generation ago, but progress towards genuine gender equality in our ranks – and our culture – has not been rapid enough. If we are serious about reforming the world of work to make it deliver for everyone, then we must be serious about reforming ourselves. We need to look, sound and feel more like today's workforce, in all of its diversity. And while a new generation of leaders and activists is coming through the ranks, it would be great to have the talents of more black and ethnic minority women (and men) at the fore.

The greatest challenge facing trade unionism is that of renewal. That's why the TUC is leading a major project to help unions to reach out to, organise and energise a new generation of young members. How we engage with young women will be critical to the project's success – unions must show they are fully attuned to their concerns and aspirations. Positioning ourselves as champions of great jobs for all – and genuine flexibility for all – will be crucial. Young and old, black and white, blue-collar and white-collar, those born in Britain and those who have chosen it as their home, trade unions must be there for working women of every background.

Ultimately the best protection any woman worker can have is a union card in her pocket. Unionised women earn more, are paid more equally, have better holidays and pensions, and are more likely to receive training than their non-union counterparts. Just as it was a century and more ago, organisation is the difference between begging and bargaining. Although our lives have changed – we bear fewer children, later in life; we have had more formal education; we have benefited from the women's suffrage and liberation movements – the need for collective organisation remains as urgent now as it ever was. As Mary Macarthur, the inspirational leader of the chainmakers, so famously put it: "Women are unorganised because they are badly paid, and poorly paid because they are unorganised."

6: THE WORLD OF WORK:
PART TWO: PROTECTING THE GAINS

Lisa Nandy MP

The world of work is changing – and women are on the frontline. More investment in skills and an economic policy based on inclusive growth would help transform their lives.

Protecting the legal safeguards for people at work will be the biggest challenge facing Labour MPs in the years ahead. And not only does Labour need to protect the gains of our last term in government. We also have to develop new policies to protect people in an economy that has moved from industrial, to post-industrial to gig, with associated changes in financial and bargaining power.

In 1997, 18 years of the systematic dismantling of trade union rights, the abolition of wage councils and widespread low pay had left many struggling with inadequate wages, childcare responsibilities and humiliation in the workplace. For young women and single parents, the situation was especially bleak.

Thirteen years later, when Labour left office a series of reforms had together made a big difference. There were initiatives that consciously sought to improve the situation of women at work – tax credits, the extension of free childcare, Sure Start centres and maternity and paternity leave. But additionally, there was wider action on rights at work, signing up to the European Social Chapter, moves to tackle abuse of agency contracts and resources put into enforcement.

The immediate priority was to deal with youth unemployment which stood at 250,000. Later the introduction of the minimum wage raised the wages of 1 million low-paid workers overnight, 70 per cent of them women. It is easy to forget how important these reforms were for women who were, and remain, disproportionately concentrated in insecure and low-paid work.

But Labour also came to power determined to shake off a long-held reputation for poor economic governance and an anti-business approach. This context was in part responsible for the reluctance to tackle emerging trends like the growing casualisation of the workforce in the interests of employers. This had profound social and economic consequences for families across the country, affecting women in particular.

As the numbers in agency work grew during Labour's time in office, increasingly workers were subject to zero-hours contracts. It is estimated that by 2020, the number of people on zero-hours contracts will stand at 1 million. Not only are women more likely to be on these contracts. But the Resolution Foundation has found that women accounted for 85 per cent of the growth in temporary agency workers since 2011.

For women, who still take on the bulk of caring responsibilities, this shift is impossible to ignore. Zero-hours workers are denied job security, the ability to borrow, to claim tax credits and childcare allowances, and suffer serious disruption to family life. In 2015 Labour rightly pledged to ban exploitative zero-hours contracts but just as important as winning new rights is having the means to exercise them. In recent years the raising of employment tribunal fees and removal of legal aid has rendered many workplace rights essentially meaningless.

Meanwhile the proportion of the workforce which is self-employed has grown. But for women who want to work for themselves, as with those on zero-hours contracts, access to free childcare entitlement, tax credits and maternity leave remains limited or out of reach. A future Labour government cannot rely simply on state regulation and extending rights at work but must also consider how to tackle wider issues such as bogus self-employment, the willingness of banks to lend to the self-employed and the availability of affordable childcare. These issues help to explain why women are less likely than men to be self-employed and almost half as likely to start their own company as men. In 2014, only 20 per cent of small and medium enterprises in the UK were majority-led by women.

Huge cuts to public services have seen the numbers of public sector workers decline since 2010. This is particularly serious for women, who are more likely to work in the sector and have felt the brunt of these job losses. A future Labour government must prioritise a renewed focus on getting women back into work, especially those who are older and have struggled to get back into the workforce after losing their jobs.

We will need a new understanding that public and private sectors are no longer monolithic. Not only do people move between them but the increase in outsourcing has left many women working within the private sector for our public services. They are less often the focus of Labour's attention.

Labour needs a wider vision for work to understand that many people who work in the private sector also offer a public service and we should celebrate, support and nurture the opportunities for people to find meaning in work wherever it exists.

Huge challenges remain. Women are three times more likely to work part-time, and much more likely to end up in certain professions: administrative and secretarial, social care, leisure and customer service sectors – which continue to be broadly low-paid. Young women apprentices are paid less, receive fewer training opportunities and are more likely to be unemployed upon completion than their male counterparts. They are hugely over-represented in health and social care, while young men are more likely to take apprenticeships in information technology, engineering and construction. These industries tend to offer higher pay and better progression routes.

There are a number of ways Labour can begin to address this. They include: raising the pay in sectors like social care where women predominate and are especially poorly paid; extending the ability of workers in those sectors to set up co-ops thus sharing a greater proportion of the rewards; introducing quotas for apprenticeships and reintroducing proper careers advice, mentoring schemes and programmes like Aim Higher that were abolished by the coalition. The most radical, and important of these reforms would be to seize the opportunity almost grasped by the Labour government and introduce a system of academic and vocational qualifications for 14 to 19-year-olds as recommended by Mike Tomlinson's working group back in 2004.

This would be a system fit for the future. We know that maths and science will be increasingly important for future jobs. We also know that automation is likely to change the jobs market significantly with a core of jobs in areas like customer service continuing to be done by humans, potentially increasingly low-paid and lacking in career progression.

In this context, we need a new vision of work as something that doesn't just build the economy but enables us to live richer, larger, more meaningful lives. Labour's explicit aim must be to give people the ability to make their own choices based on their own priorities of family, work, and income. This means improving workers' rights, at a time when we are withdrawing from the European Union, the source of what-ever progress was made during our last period in opposition. The hard Brexit being pursued by the Tories carries a real risk of comprehensive deregulation of our labour markets.

We also need to argue for investing in skills, reforming the education system and rebuilding the middle tier of jobs so people no longer get stuck in low-paid jobs with limited prospects. We should pursue an economic policy based on inclusive growth so we share equally in the proceeds and don't have to leave the welfare state to do so much heavy lifting, pitting the working and middle classes against one another and leaving us all poorer. A system that works in the interests of labour not capital would change women's lives, and in doing so build us a stronger, fairer, happier country.

7: EQUALITY: BUILDING A MORE TOLERANT BRITAIN

Angela Eagle MP and Vera Baird

In the 20 years since 1997, remarkable progress has been made on equality. But of late the mood has been shifting and progressives need to work to protect the more tolerant country that Labour helped to create.

"We live in a world that sometimes seems to be changing too fast for comfort. Old certainties crumbling. Traditional values falling away. People are bewildered... And people ask: 'Where's it going? Why has it happened?' And above all: 'How can we stop it?'".
– John Major, 1993 Conservative party conference

"I do not want an old social order. I want a new one with rules for today... In any young country, the talents of all are allowed to flourish. There should be no discrimination in our young country on grounds of disability, gender, age, sexuality or race."
– Tony Blair, 1995 Labour party conference

The contrast between the two visions of Britain presented by Labour and the Tories in the mid-1990s could not have been starker.

Behind John Major's seemingly anodyne plea for 'traditional values' lay a nostalgia for a less socially liberal country, a less diverse and tolerant one. Despite the moralising tone of his speech to the 1993 Tory conference, there was not a single reference to fighting discrimination and prejudice, no sense of a crusade to defend the rights of minorities as well as those of the majority. No sense that the time had come to end the historic wrongs done to women, the 51 per cent of the population who faced endemic discrimination, narrowing their life chances and following them from the cradle to the grave.

But in the world outside Tory-run Westminster, attitudes had begun to change. Women had moved into the workplace in their millions and they were increasingly represented by trade unions who had reformed their bargaining agendas to better reflect women's everyday concerns: child care, maternity rights, time off for caring responsibilities, career breaks, parental leave. This change was picked up and reflected quickly in Labour's internal democratic procedures and it began to be reflected too in the agenda of the annual conference.

In contrast to John Major, Tony Blair had his finger on the pulse of Britain in the 90s, identifying the UK as a 'young country' that was increasingly progressive and outward-looking, and with little time for passing judgement on the basis of gender, race, sexuality or disability. And it was this analysis which caught the public mood and helped sweep Labour to its historic landslide victory on 1 May 1997.

If Britain was becoming a more liberal, tolerant place during the 1980s and 1990s, then you would be forgiven for doubting it based on some of the legislation in place, or indeed some of the views held by senior Tory ministers. It is worth reminding ourselves which laws were still on the statute book when Labour came to power, and which laws were conspicuous by their absence.

The notorious Section 28 had been introduced in 1988, stating that councils should not 'intentionally promote homosexuality or publish material with the intention of promoting homosexuality or pretend family relationships' in their schools or other areas of their work. There was no mechanism for same-sex couples to obtain legal recognition for their relationship, and the age of consent for gay men was 21 as opposed to 16 for everyone else.

There was no Human Rights Act or Equality and Human Rights Commission. The gender pay gap still stood at 27 per cent and the Equal Pay Act was more honoured in the breach than the observance. It took an average of 10 years to bring a successful demand for equal pay, and even if successful it did not apply generally. Meanwhile there were just 60 female MPs in the House of Commons. And before 1997 there had only ever been seven black and minority ethnic MPs in the whole post-war history of our parliament, and only two out LGBT MPs. Parliament was spectacularly access-unfriendly, as Anne Begg discovered when she, a wheelchair user, was elected in 1997.

If the legislation from this period had not kept pace with public opinion, then the rhetoric of Tory ministers hadn't either. Social security secretary Peter Lilley entertained the 1992 Tory conference with his 'little list' song, declaring his priority to root out "those who make up bogus claims" and "young ladies who get pregnant just to jump the housing queue".

In 1998 former Conservative minister Norman Tebbit said gay men in public life – and therefore 'in a position to do each other favours' – should be 'outed', and should be barred from becoming home secretary. Eight years earlier Tebbit had made headlines with his infamous 'cricket test': "A large proportion of Britain's Asian population fail to pass the cricket test. Which side do they cheer for? It's an interesting test. Are you still harking back to where you came from or where you are?" There was also much baiting by the media and government ministers of 'loony lefties' who dared to argue for equal rights for all including LGBT people. From some of the comments you would hear on the doorstep, there was no doubt that the attack was effective.

Labour's determination in 1997 to combat discrimination and pursue a rigorous equalities agenda must be viewed as a brave reaffirmation of our values as a party. Such determination had been punished in previous general elections. Some were more enthusiastic to pursue it than others but it was prioritised in the end because of the number of determined believers in the cause of equality in the parliamentary Labour party and in the trade unions. And a quick glance at Labour's record during the first term of government reveals just how fierce this determination was.

In 1997 the Disability Rights Task Force was established to advise government on how to meet Labour's manifesto commitment to secure enforceable civil rights for disabled people, resulting in the establishment of the Disability Rights Commission two years later. The following year the Human Rights Act was passed, giving domestic legal effect to the provisions of the European Convention on Human Rights. Article 14 provided a right to enjoy any other convention right without discrimination "on any ground such as sex, race, colour, language, religion, political or other opinion, national or social origin, association with a national minority, property, birth or other status".

A number of employment regulations entered the statute books which made it unlawful to discriminate on the grounds of sexual orientation, religion or disability.

Statutory paternity pay was introduced and maternity pay extended. Women would disproportionately benefit from Labour's numerous measures to assist the low-paid, such as the minimum wage. Child tax credits boosted women's incomes, especially for single mothers. Parliament itself was becoming a less male-dominated environment with the election of 101 female Labour MPs in 1997.

This trend continued throughout Labour's three terms. Civil partnerships were introduced for same-sex couples and Section 28 was repealed after massive effort at the third time of asking. The age of consent was also equalised but not before the Parliament Act had to be invoked to overcome the fierce resistance of the House of Lords.

A closer look at some of these measures gives an insight into the challenges faced by the Labour government and ministers' determination to introduce change.

Sexual Offences laws needed rewriting from scratch. It should be remembered that throughout their time in office the Tories did nothing to make rape in marriage a crime. That changed only because the courts took unilateral action – and that was not until two years after the departure of the first woman prime minister.

Complaining of rape brought, as a matter of course, cross-examination about previous sexual behaviour, real or invented. It was always irrelevant but hugely prejudicial and a deterrent to taking a case.

That had to stop and the issue shone a light on where Tory 'justice' had left other victims; older people, the young, people with learning disabilities and those made unequal by the impact of the crime in itself. The 418 Labour MPs were determined to put the wellbeing of their grassroots constituents at the forefront of reform. By 1999 sexual history in rape cases had been vastly cut back and vulnerable and intimidated witnesses were protected at the heart

of the trial. Legislation was painstakingly reshaped, equalising sexual offences regardless of orientation, eliminating
discrimination between straight and gay sexual activity
and modernising concepts such as legal consent.

Tackling domestic violence had been neglected. In 2002
a female Conservative MP conceded that domestic violence
had never been mentioned at their party conference. Nor
had it appeared in the outgoing Major government's manifesto in 1997, a year in which there were more than three
million incidents, with 90 per cent of them against women.
We prioritised arrest and prosecution, toughening the stance
against perpetrators and creating special domestic violence
courts, where magistrates were trained in the dynamics of
coercive domestic abuse and prosecutors were all special-
ists. The very name of the court sent out a strong message.
There was a new kind of independent adviser, both supporting the victim and representing her interests with the
justice agencies.

Resource for refuges was in short supply until our
Supporting People fund went out to local councils, earmarked
for specialist housing. In short, we designed model public
services, effective to tackle domestic abuse in and out of
court and which still work today – where Tory austerity
policy hasn't wiped them out.

Conservative neglect had also left the law adrift.
Domestic abusers who killed their partners could rely on
an ancient claim of being provoked beyond self-control,
blaming the victim for their own loss of temper. This
got convictions downgraded and sentences shortened. But
victims who struck out in fear, following years of abuse
were not driven by temper and had no such defence. The
law merely convicted abusers of manslaughter while victims
became murderers, imprisoned for life. Key appeal cases like
that of Emma Humphreys showed the need for law that

was fair to differing gender responses and women ministers worked up a radical restructure of homicide law.

Anti-discrimination law was left fragmented, inconsistent and out of date by 18 years of Conservative rule. Some of the strands protected such as race had broader equalities than others such as gender and age and some such as LGBT hardly featured at all.

In other words and unsurprisingly, the Tories ran Britain on a hierarchy of equalities.

The advent of the Human Rights Act raised the question of a Human Rights Commission, inviting a review of the three separate equalities commissions then struggling to implement this maze. By 2007 they were merged into the Equality and Human Rights Commission, seen as a key forerunner to implementing root and branch reform of equality law itself. There followed probably the widest programme of stakeholder outreach ever undertaken by a UK government, with thousands of responses contributing to the equalities and discrimination law reviews on which the new law was grounded.

The Equality Act 2010 was, therefore, in every way, the people's legislation. It went on to embrace everyone. The duty it put onto public authorities to mainstream equality and advance opportunity includes, at a strategic level, reducing unequal outcomes caused by poverty. In the House of Commons on 24 April 2009, Harriet Harman, then women and equalities minister, said: "Everyone has the right to be treated fairly and everyone should enjoy the opportunity to fulfil their potential. No-one should suffer the indignity of discrimination – to be told you're old so you're past it, to be overlooked because of a disability, to be excluded because of the colour of your skin to be harassed because you are gay or to be paid unfairly because you are a woman... But we all recognise that discrimination can happen, not just because of your age, gender or race. It can also be because of your family background, your socio-economic status or class".

The Tory response, from Theresa May, was to propose a move that would have killed the bill stone dead. She said that the House of Commons should refuse the bill a second reading – it was 'unnecessarily onerous on business'. When asked to name anyone who supported voting it down, the Tories could only refer to the Society Against Political Correctness. As it moved from the Commons, May attacked it again in the House of Lords with a three-clause alternative Equality Bill, speedily despatched by Labour peers.

A magnificent team effort got this great Labour bill into law before the 2010 general election making it diffi-cult for the Tories to abandon it. But, true to Theresa May's stance then, they have implemented just the bare bones. They have failed – of course – to implement the clause on socio-economic equality, with no gender pay gap reporting and without banning multiple discrimina-tion, such as that against older women or younger black males. Our Equality Act honoured the struggles of many people and it was Labour who saw them fulfilled.

Conclusion

Labour's general election victory in 1997, and the euphoric mood that accompanied it, now seem like a very long time ago. Politics in the 1990s was suffused with a sense that social progress was inevitable, and that the barriers which had for so long divided society on the basis of gender, race, disability and sexuality were being inexorably eroded. This assumption now seems uncomfortably distant and, with the election of Trump and stirrings of the far right in this country, the zeitgeist of 2017 is now arguably moving in the opposite direction. The backlash has well and truly begun, and it is clear that those of us who believe in equality before the law have a huge battle on our hands to keep the gains we have made.

The mood has darkened in recent years, with 'go home' vans and 'breaking point' posters, a divisive form of rhetoric around immigration legitimised by the rise of Ukip, and the disturbing increase in hate crime after Brexit. Tory cuts have blazed through the public sector with scant regard for the consequences for the most deprived people in the country. An uncaring system penalises those with disabilities through cost-cutting assessments, while those on benefits are vilified as 'scroungers' and 'skivers'.

And yet, despite all these threats to the more decent, tolerant society Labour did so much to shape, it is important to remember that much of the Labour government's legacy still stands. Landmark pieces of legislation, including the Equality Act, remain, albeit watered down by the Tories. For now the Human Rights Act remains in place. The coalition government's introduction of gay marriage would surely not have happened had it not been for Labour's reforms and a shift in the terms of the debate, which helped drag the Tories into the 21st century. It is perhaps difficult to imagine senior Tories now making pronouncements comparable to Lilley's 'little list' or Tebbit's cricket test.

There are many who seek to traduce the record of the last Labour government. In the areas of equality and diversity we need to be especially vocal about our achievements in government. The long list of Labour's equalities reforms should not just be viewed as individual achievements, but as a sea change in direction which made Britain a more progressive country. It is this overarching direction which highlights how much a Labour government can achieve, and how much is at stake when we remain out of office for extended periods, giving the Tories a licence to steer the country in the opposite direction.

So let's remember that we made a real difference and be proud that our party changed equality for the better for future generations. Let's fight to win the right to do it again.

8: BEYOND BRITAIN: WORKING WITH PARTNERS WORLDWIDE

Tulip Siddiq MP with assistance from Margaret Beckett MP

The international aid budget is under assault from those on the right who argue we should be spending at home, not abroad. It's more important than ever, then that we herald Labour's internationalist record, transforming the lives of the world's poorest women, improving education and health and tackling gendered violence.

In these turbulent times, as Britain embarks upon a future outside the European Union, and Theresa May appears intent on appeasing the new US administration, Labour's commitment to internationalism is more important than ever.

The choice between globalism and nationalism has never been so destructive. In so many ways, the sharp divisions outlined in our 1997 manifesto, between those who wish 'to retreat into isolationism and protectionism', and those 'who believe in internationalism and engagement' have become more acute with time.

The consequences of an isolationist and protectionist future would be devastating for women at home and around the globe. It would not only put a halt to progress being made, but it would also roll back the framework of support for women built over the course of our proud history.

And it is a proud history, full of inspirational women who have left an indelible mark on the global stage. Their achievements must not be glossed over, not least when celebrating the very real impact of Labour's most recent period of government.

Labour's historic internationalism

To understand Labour's internationalist history, take the example of Ada Salter, Labour's first female mayor, whose public campaigns for child and maternal health comfortably predated efforts later adopted by international institutions.

Or take Barbara Castle, responsible with Harold Wilson in 1964 for creating the Ministry for Overseas Development. Most famous for her work on the Equal Pay Act of 1970, Barbara instituted the belief that combatting global poverty should be a priority of British foreign policy. Her visionary commitment to development has become a hallmark of Britain's approach to international relations, and accepted across mainstream political parties.

And take Judith Hart, who devoted her political life to fighting poverty and injustice. As another female minister for overseas development, she was a fierce opponent of apartheid in South Africa and of Pinochet's atrocities in Chile. She was also famously the first minister in overseas development to refine pro-poor development policy, saying the goal was to direct aid to the "poorest people in the poorest countries".

These women inspired Labour's future policymaking, especially for the whole raft of female leaders who would follow.

International challenges in 1997

Labour's later involvement in Iraq and Afghanistan has inevitably become the focus of debate, but the notion that Labour transformed the lives of millions of women across the globe while in government is indisputable. The establishment of the Department for International Development, led by a secretary of state of full cabinet rank, initiated a revolution in gendered policymaking that improved the lives of women worldwide.

Whether in peacekeeping efforts, climate change initiatives, or poverty alleviation programmes, Labour normalised the consideration of gender within major development issues and set about dismantling structural inequalities that had been allowed to flourish for centuries.

The scale of the challenges faced by the world's poorest women in 1997 cannot be overstated. The Human Development Report of that year reveals that women accounted for almost 70 per cent of the 1.3 billion people in extreme poverty, living on less than $1 a day. Of the 840 million illiterate adults, two-thirds were women. Nearly 800 million people lacked access to basic health services, and women were at least ten times more likely than they are now to die of causes related to pregnancy and childbirth. There was a clear need to help women to go through pregnancy and childbirth more safely, and to protect women from sexual violence. More than 1 billion people lacked access to safe water, and women in developing countries would spend hours every day travelling to find water. An estimated 158 million children aged under five were malnourished.

The fast pace of globalisation that improved living standards in the west throughout the 1980s and early 1990s barely registered in the lives of the world's poorest women. Post-independence growth in many African countries had collapsed and unsustainable debts incurred by countries in Latin America and the Caribbean had entirely inhibited progress. Helping those who had previously lacked access to decent health, education and employment was at the top of Labour's agenda.

Achievements of Labour in government

In 1997, we were confronted with a need to refocus international development to tackle the reality that women were disproportionately affected by poverty. This is made clear in DfID's first white paper.

Claire Short, the first secretary of state for the department, immediately set about linking Britain's support for national development plans and gender equality. She said: "Poor women are frequently doubly disadvantaged in access to services, in access to and control over economic resources and in participation in public life. This perpetuates gender inequality."

In 2017, this may not seem so revolutionary, but making combatting poverty the priority in the battle to overcome gender inequality marked a significant break from preceding orthodoxies.

During our years in government, Labour's mission to put international development at the heart of national policy thinking had clear and lasting results for women globally.

And no matter how often one hears them, the figures are staggering. The tripling of the aid budget and the commitment to spending 0.7 per cent of gross national income were not simply targets to enable a social democratic party to feel good about itself, but a move that took 3 million people, permanently, out of poverty each year. By putting women's rights and wellbeing at the heart of our development programme, we helped millions around the world build a future free from suffering.

Our transformative attitude toward combatting domestic violence, at home and abroad, made Britain a leader in campaigning against gender-based violence. Between 1997 and 2010, the Labour government fundamentally changed the way governments viewed and responded to domestic violence, challenging the perception that it was a 'private' issue.

Our work on maternal mortality produced particularly outstanding results. In Pakistan, our support for initiatives to increase the number of midwives helped to prevent 15,000 mothers' deaths. In India, between 2006 and 2010, Labour government funding created nearly 2,000 health facilities to provide specialist new-born care. We ensured that over 11,000 public health facilities were functional in India's rural areas, training more than 540,000 community-based health workers. In Ghana, UK funding supported a 28 per cent reduction in child mortality rates, achieved by ensuring that nine out of every 10 pregnant women attended at least one antenatal clinic. A similar strategy was applied in south central Somalia, where we set up 34 primary health care clinics serving 500,000 people.

In those years Labour also recognised that aid in the form of education was a primary route to reducing gender inequality.

By 2010, the UK had the largest bilateral aid programme with Bangladesh. We helped more than 1 million Bangladeshi children obtain primary education, building 15,000 classrooms and recruiting 14,000 teachers. Similarly, the £1bn given to support urban regeneration in India helped bring more than 20 million more children into school and established 250,000 new schools.

In Africa, our biggest advances in educational equality were in Nigeria and Ghana. We worked with the Ghanaian government and local civil society organisations to ensure that school completion increased to 90 per cent by 2010 and that equal numbers of boys and girls attended primary school. In Nigeria, we provided particular support to female teacher trainees from rural areas, where there are very few female teachers.

As with education and healthcare, Labour offered support to women around the world through measures to improve criminal justice systems and increase governmental accountability.

Through the efforts of DfID and the Foreign Office supporting stronger governance and security services, we delivered leaps in safety for women in the Caribbean and South America. In Jamaica, our support helped to reduce murder rates in the Dunkirk and Matthews Lane areas by more than 90 per cent in just three years. In Guyana, we concentrated on strengthening security and justice through support to the police and through the reintegration of criminal deportees.

Equally important in our successive terms in office was the recognition from ministers that the support that we offered to the developing world would need to be sustainable. This remains a particularly pressing challenge for progressive parties, whose defence of the international aid budget is so often criticised as being symptomatic of misplaced spending priorities.

Our efforts in government prioritised women's economic empowerment as a key to sustainable development. Through debt-cancelling measures and anti-corruption programmes, Labour eased the burden on countries whose arrears prevented improvements to the lives of the poorest women.

At the Gleneagles summit in 2005, we led the international campaign to cancel 100 per cent of multilateral debts, and subsequently launched a governance and transparency fund providing resources to local civil society groups to improve governance and increase accountability in poor countries.

It would be remiss not to mention Labour's approach to climate change as a marker of significant progress in those years. Under our chairmanship of the UN Security Council, Labour embraced and championed the position that climate change was a matter of peace and security, not least for women.

Previously, climate change had been the preserve of other UN bodies, including the Framework Convention on Climate Change. However, we stood firm in asserting that major changes to the world's physical landmass during this century could lead to border and maritime dispute. Further we argued, the risk that parts of the world could become uninhabitable was a profound security concern.

At the heart of this approach was the awareness that women farmers account for up to 85 per cent of all food production in developing countries. These women were dependent for their livelihood on resources that are threatened by climate change. Yet women subsistence farmers are often excluded from decision-making over the use of land so essential to their livelihoods.

Labour's promotion of the rights of rural women pushed the gendered consequences of climate change from the fringes to the mainstream of global public consciousness.

Elsewhere, in peacekeeping, Labour's achievements may not have specifically been *for women* but efforts were certainly led *by women* and of great consequence *to women* in the affected countries.

As the first female Northern Ireland secretary, the late, great Mo Mowlam, was a key architect of the Good Friday Agreement. History will rightly remember the reconciliation agreement signed between men whose lives had been dominated by the armed struggle. But those involved in the process overwhelmingly attributed the success of negotiations to Mo's direct and unconventional approach.

In Sierra Leone's civil war, young girls were routinely captured and forced to take up arms. Organisations such as Human Rights Watch and Médecins sans Frontières detail the thousands of accounts of rape and sexual abuse, which was commonly used as a weapon of war. It is no surprise, therefore, that Tony Blair counts the decision to intervene in that civil war amongst one of his most important. Essential to the rebuilding of the country post-civil war was Baroness Valerie Amos, then minister for Africa. She co-ordinated the financial and logistical support to Sierra Leone's truth and reconciliation commission, aiming to create impartial historical records of the conflict and recognising for the first time the use of rape and sexual violence as a weapon of war.

To recall the huge array of achievements in international development throughout our time in government, and the women responsible for them, is not to whitewash failures, or to be content with where things were left.

Labour's military interventions in Iraq and Afghanistan were divisive, and nobody would dare to suggest that our successes 'put to bed' global poverty, or to deny the scale to which it continues to exist. However, when making the case for a Labour government to the electorate, we need to assert the successes of those years, especially in the current contagion of retreat from internationalism.

Challenges since 2010

But if we're to inspire a new generation of global women, we have also to confront the challenges that have emerged since we left power, or that continued despite the progress. Unequal access to education, barriers to healthcare and unfair criminal justice systems still exist, not least across the Commonwealth.

We are also faced with the growing reality that we must compensate where our most trusted allies, especially the USA, are resiling from their commitments to women's rights.

The new US President Donald Trump began his term in office by signing an executive order that revived the so-called 'Mexico City policy.' Instituted in 2004, under the last Republican administration of President George W Bush, this policy prevented all NGOs that accepted US funding from providing information or counselling for abortion care, or promoting awareness of the benefits of legal reform. This compromised the work of many organisations and threatened to adversely affect DfID programmes. So the Labour government then provided the funding to fill the void.

President Trump's memorandum extends the policy, restricting a whole series of activities, and includes denying information on abortion to women supported by international development organisations. Labour must speak to our previous efforts and effectively challenge the government to step in and replace the funding.

Similar interventions will be required for countries where we have more complicated diplomatic relationships, especially Russia.

At the time of writing, a bill to decriminalise some forms of domestic violence has just been passed by the Duma, Russia's parliament. The proposal suggests that a first 'offence', or act of violence, should not be considered criminal, and punishment limited to a fine or community service. The ANNA National Centre for the Prevention of Violence notes that in Russia, 40 women a day, or 14,000 a year, die from violence at the hands of their partners. Since the law was passed, there are already reports that domestic violence has more than doubled in Yekaterinburg, Russia's fourth largest city.

As a party we should reassert our international standing on women's rights, and oppose the downgrading of gender-based crimes.

Challenging our allies and adversaries will be all the more difficult given the sustained attacks on the international aid budget by right wing media and populist ideologues. In their line of fire is DfID, at the frontline of the battle against global gender inequality.

Labour must act to honour our own history, and protect the world's poorest people by rejecting the attacks on the progressive cornerstone of British international policy. We especially need to challenge the false dichotomies of 'help abroad or help at home' and must push the government to maintain international aid spending.

Most recently, following a tranche of immigration orders by President Trump, our government seems to be following suit by cancelling its commitment to admitting child refugees. In making the case for a more compassionate approach, it is indisputable that Labour women have led the way.

The late Jo Cox MP was relentless. She was at the forefront of the response to the Syrian crisis setting up a parliamentary group on Syria in 2015 on the plight of refugees and campaigning for the government to do more to end the conflict in the region. In one of her final speeches in the Commons, Jo said she would "risk life and limb" if her own "two precious babies" were subject to the horrors of the Syrian civil war. She spoke for many of us when she called for "brave and bold" action to support child refugees.

Seven years on from our time in government, recalling triumphs can serve as a rallying point to combat historic gender inequalities. We also need to meet the challenges that lie in wait. For that we need to build a progressive alliance with women in left of centre parties in Europe and globally. We live in an uncertain world, but there can be no excuse for any British government abandoning its commitment to creating a world in which anyone can access the same opportunities, regardless of gender.

CONCLUSION: KICKING AWAY
THE STUMBLING BLOCKS

Jess Phillips MP

The conclusion to this collection is not a conclusion at all. The push for gender equality and a woman's role in politics or at the top table – or in fact any table other than the one in the kitchen – is far from concluded.

Before I talk of the challenges ahead and the fights of the future, I want to reflect first on the question of what the 101 Labour women elected in 1997 did for my generation. From where I'm sitting the answer is: everything.

I was 16 years old in 1997 and 29 in 2010 when Labour left office. From my childhood to my womanhood, a Labour government was in place. I went to university during those years, got my first job, bought my first house, got married, had both my children and nursed my nan and grandad and then my mother who later died of cancer. Tax credits, free nursery places, nursery vouchers, my local Sure Start, investment in the public and third sectors where both my husband and I worked, my children's savings accounts, my nan's care workers, her attendance allowance, my maternity leave which had improved again by the time my second baby was born, my husband's paternity leave, the charities, hospitals and hospices who helped my family as my mother deteriorated, the list of things those women rose to their feet from their green benches to demand for girls like me meant everything. So many possible stumbling blocks for my potential kicked out of the way by Labour women in a Labour government.

For my mother's generation none of these things existed, and without them, today would look very different. But a friend of mine who worked for the local council recently packed in her job: the pressure of dwindling resources and changing schedules meant work just couldn't fit in with the other demands on her life. She too has two children and a poorly mother. The stumbling blocks are being shuffled back into place.

We may have a woman prime minister in Theresa May, but unless during her premiership women actually advance, her gender will be irrelevant. Women's leadership is not the end in itself: it is part of the struggle to improve the lives of all. When I talk about trying to get more women into politics, people tell me that the representation of women in high office is feminism for the middle classes. I'd politely point to the clear effect on my life of women with power and to the words of Leymah Gbowee who won the Nobel peace prize for her work with women in Liberia. When asked what single thing we could do to improve life for the poorest, most abused women of the world, she answered: "More women in power." So they can take that argument up with her.

The world has changed since 1997, and women in politics seem to be making some steady if slow progress towards equalising the numbers. Parliament has changed and although I have only been here since 2015 I think there has been a softening or a feminising of the place in the past 20 years. The hours of sitting are better (if still not great) for parents of young children and new babies. Children often roam the halls and even the voting lobbies of the Palace of Westminster. I note that the Tories make a concerted effort to ensure that there are women in the chamber to make sure they don't seem wholly male – which they still very much are when you do a body count. The Labour party is so near gender parity that this is not something we have to work to achieve.

I think the tone and pace of the place have changed as more women have taken their seats. People readily speak of their personal experiences, their mental health problems, their personal bereavements, their fears and in the most unprecedented cases their own rape. Opening the doors to all those women all those years ago and fighting to maintain and improve that standard has brought all lives into the building and moved the place on from being a home for one kind of person, in one kind of suit, with one kind of life.

But as the palace softened, I'm afraid to say that the world hardened for women in politics. I don't for a second think that the animosity myself and my colleagues face for being women with opinions didn't exist for the women of 1997 and the handfuls who came before. I'm certain that it did. But the dawn of internet technology has brought that animosity into our homes and into every minute of our lives. The animosity is no longer confined to private poison pen letters only to be shared with the police. It is now writ large for all to see, beaming a terrible message out to women who might be daring themselves to give this thing a go.

For young women today, the intimacies of their childhood relationships, their youthful misdemeanours are all filed up in the cloud for people to use against them. Instead of opening up these clouds and letting it rain real people with real lives over Westminster, I fear the atmosphere will affect the type of women who want to put themselves forward.

So it is for the women in the PLP to challenge this and to take on the extra work of mentoring and encouraging young women. Each and every woman in the PLP has three roles: being a local champion and managing a difficult, usually marginal, constituency; operating as a 'just as good as the boys are' Westminster legislator; and also acting as the feminist activist tasked with keeping politics open for everybody.

This pamphlet sets out some of the hows of our story. How those Labour women MPs kicked away the stumbling blocks when we got into government in 1997. Wallet to purse economics, ending pensioner poverty, tackling child poverty. And how a new generation of Labour women, in opposition for the time being, is sizing up the new barriers to equality here and around a smaller but meaner world.

Our challenge now is to keep up the pace and to make sure we are not just window dressing, a tool to endear people to politics but not to change it. I don't want the women of the PLP to just be peddled out to win women's votes. Women politicians must be presented as the people who can solve everybody's problems.

I'm not suggesting for a second that we should stop focusing on women's rights – in fact the opposite. I truly believe that gender equality is the key to solving so many of our current national challenges. Especially the biggest challenge of all: "It's the economy stupid!" The UK has a productivity problem and frankly that is not a surprise, because when we talk about infrastructure, or industrial strategy in this country we conveniently forget half the population. When we talk about building roads and railways, do we stop to consider how many women will be employed in these jobs? We plan for mass house building and invest big in this, but we know only one per cent of construction jobs go to the sisters.

Of course we should invest in employment in our infrastructure. I was recently accused of being snotty about these jobs by a Tory minister when I had asked if we could invest in women's employment. But I'm not being snotty: I'm just begging for people with my chromosomal make-up to get these jobs that have been denied to them before.

Where is the Tory government's strategy to think about gender when it considers the skills gap? We hear about connectivity and getting people working in a digital world, about laying cables and planning routes to work but there's never a recognition that half of us would be far more industrious if only we could get out of the house. They never look at our productivity problem and think that maybe investing in universal childcare might be an idea. Or that an industrial strategy for care might save the millions of working hours lost to stress and mental health ailments. Such a strategy might mean older women, who suffer the worst of the gender pay gap would not have to work part-time in order to care for their older relatives. Women have been workers for centuries but no industrial strategy I ever read seems to have noticed. The lack of women in the line-up for the northern powerhouse conference was a case in point.

The reason the women of 1997 saved my life was not because they handed me benefits, or 15 hours of free childcare to give me a break. It is because they allowed me to get out of my house and become something. Young women being something is not just good in itself, it's good for us all. What is lost in missed contributions to both the Treasury and society must run to billions of pounds. Thousands of missed opportunities for innovation, lifesaving medicine, beautiful things and technical revolutions. What could have been if only we'd thought to remember the women keeps me awake at night. What have we missed?

If the women elected in 1997 taught us anything it is that women's voices in parliament make stuff happen for women in the world. It was not just me who benefited from those years. All my friends did too, and in turn their families, their husbands, their children, the local shops where we lived, the travel industry, our local schools, and our older and infirm relatives. The benefits of our freedom were shared with all.

For Us All
Redesigning social
security, for the 2020s

Andrew Harrop

For Us All examines the reform of social security
for children and working-age adults, in the 2020s.
For six years of the Cameron government, 'austerity'
dominated all discussion of benefit policies. Now it is
time to turn a page and start to consider the long-term
future of social security, as part of a strategic agenda
for raising British living standards. Social security
for pensioners is now on a strong and sustainable
footing. But the system for non-pensioners will be
worse in 2020 than it was in 2010 – and will carry on
getting worse, unless policy changes.
The report examines the reason why current policies
are failing and then assesses improvements to means-
tested, contributory and universal benefits as well as
private support, proposing that the end-point might
be a tiered system with elements of them all.

JOIN THE FABIANS TODAY

Join us and receive at least four pamphlets or books a year as well as our quarterly magazine, 'Fabian Review'.

I'd like to become a Fabian

Standard Rate: £3.50 per month/£42 per annum
Reduced Rate (unwaged): £1.75 per month/£21 per annum

Name	Date of birth
Address	Postcode
Email	
Telephone	

Instruction to Bank   Originator's ID: 971666

Bank/building society name	
Address	**DIRECT Debit**
Acct holder(s)	Postcode
Acct no.	Sort code

I instruct you to pay direct debits from my account at the request of the
Fabian Society. The instruction is subject to the safeguards of the Direct Debit Guarantee.

| Signature | Date |

Return to:
Fabian Society Membership
FREEPOST RTEG – XLTU – AEJX
61 Petty France, London SW1H 9EU